Walks With A Three-Legged Cat

Ken Homer. (EKH)

Walks With A Three-Legged Cat

& Other Observations

By **Ken Homer**

edited by
Stuart Kinney & Ross Kinney

illustrated by
Michael McEwing

published by
Chapel Street Editions
in association with
The Carleton County Historical Society

Published by
Chapel Street Editions in association with
The Carleton County Historical Society

Chapel Street Editions
150 Chapel Street
Woodstock, New Brunswick E7M 1H4
www.chapelstreeteditions.com

The Carleton County Historical Society
128 Connell Street
Woodstock, New Brunswick E7M 1L5
www.cchsnb.ca

ISBN 978-1-988299-26-6

Library and Archives Canada Cataloguing in Publication

Title: Walks with a three-legged cat & other observations / by Ken Homer / edited by Stuart Kinney & Ross Kinney ; illustrated by Michael McEwing.

Other titles: Essays. Selections | Walks with a three-legged cat and other observations

Names: Homer, Ken, 1915-2003 author. | Kinney, Stuart, 1959- editor. | Kinney, Ross, 1992- editor.

Identifiers: Canadiana 2019019135X | ISBN 9781988299266 (softcover)

Subjects: LCSH: Homer, Ken.

Classification: LCC PS8565.O6507 A6 2019 | DDC C814/.54—dc23

The woodcut on the cover and the illustrations that preceed each season of the book are by Michael McEwing.

The photographs were provided by the Estate of Ken Homer (EKH), by Mary Bernard (MB), by The Carleton County Historical Society (CCHS), and by the Provincial Archives of New Brunswick (PANB).

The painting on the back cover is *The Farmhouse* by Ron Smith, 1961.

The map was created by Stuart Kinney and Brendan Helmuth with materials from the L.P. Fisher Public Library Archive and Wikimedia Commons.

Book design by Brendan Helmuth.

This book is dedicated to
Keith Helmuth, who tends our cultural garden; and
the Wolastoq, whose bounty sustains our heritage.

The Table of Contents

Radio Noon Sept 14/79

Each year when mid-September
comes around there are certain times
of day when changes in the quality
of light itself prophesy
autumn's imminent
arrival as surely as the turning
of the leaves.

~~And~~ Each year about this time
the thought comes to me that if I
were an artist I would be working
intensively ~~[illegible]~~, dawn to dusk,
from now until the falling of the
snow.

In late September there
is such variety – the more
noticeable since the sun rises
at a reasonable ~~hour~~ and we're
~~[illegible]~~ conscious of the whole range
of rich illumination from
early morning until sunset.

The other day, beyond the
morning mist, I watched the ~~[illegible]~~ glow
of eastern light intensify until
suddenly, ~~the sky~~ white clouds drifting
higher above the river and the hills
changed to a roseate pink
which spread and deepened

Handwritten radio script, 1979. (PANB)

Looking For What There Is To See

A Foreword

The Beginning

In the 1970s and '80s, Ken Homer broadcast a series of weekly essays which were heard throughout the Maritimes on the CBC's daily audio potpourri known as *Radio Noon*. Like the show itself, the essays featured a wide array of topics including commentary on the flora and fauna of western New Brunswick, local and national history, current and cultural affairs, literature, and music — in short, they reflected the eclectic interests of their author. Not surprisingly, what was of interest to Homer was also of interest to his wide audience, and his weekly musings came to be anticipated keenly by listeners.

Covering a period of approximately six years and comprising more than 250 episodes, this series of Ken Homer's radio essays served to enhance the local and regional acclaim of this CBC journalist as an historian, conservationist, naturalist, teacher, and commentator. With Homer's dulcet-toned voice, erudite diction, omnivorous curiosity, and deep literary knowledge, along with his quaint sign-off — "This is Ken Homer in Upper Woodstock"— the broadcasts were treasured for their ability to convey simple truths about the world around us and the people we encounter in it. They were homilies for a secular world.

In 2014, when Chapel Street Editions (CSE) announced the re-publishing of the entire George Frederick Clarke oeuvre and its interest in other writers from the community's history, it made sense to consider a selection of Homer's essays for publication. His place among local historians and literary figures, and as a prominent member of the Clarke household, made a nice fit. CSE's publisher and managing editor, Keith Helmuth, expressed immediate and unqualified enthusiasm.

Thus, the idea of the present volume germinated.

The Book

Through conversation with Homer's son, Stephen, CSE received permission to produce a volume of essays from the manuscripts deposited in the Provincial Archives of New Brunswick. It was there in early 2017 we first encountered boxes laden with hundreds of letter-sized pages of the yellowish newsprint common to newsrooms of Homer's era. A few essays had been typewritten, but most of the pages were covered in his spidery, wandering scrawl. Though evidently legible enough to serve as his script, many passages often proved nearly indecipherable to us as first-time readers, a challenge heightened by Homer's frequent marginal and interlinear emendations (signs of the mind at work!). We also came upon the occasional hole in a page—the apparent effect of an encounter with mice, perhaps in the attic of the Clarke house where his papers had been stored.

We dove into reading and cataloguing the output to make our selection for this volume. The original scripts served as our primary source and were verified by listening to the archived audio of original broadcasts. After this confirmation, minor edits for clarity and consistency were made without troubling any of the content. In addition, in those instances where Homer left an essay untitled, we supplied a descriptive heading that seemed to hew to his sensibilities.

Quickly, a clearer view of Homer's interests and style appeared and the work started to impose its own form on our publication. On the one hand, we could not capture all his distinctive qualities. Homer's voice and delivery leave a great impression on his listeners, but his oratorical style cannot be fully reflected in the written form. On the other hand, we followed Homer where we found him: moving in stride with the seasons, often meandering through tangents and side stories, but inevitably reconciled with his point of departure. Through it all, curiosity remained his engine.

We've tried to reflect these aspects of Homer's personality in the selection of essays chosen for this book. They are arranged by season because Homer often drew inspiration from the "seasonal signs in the world of nature"—including the chores, preoccupations, and celebrations of each month. We try to show the variety of his writing, how wide a net he cast on history, and how enthusiastically he was willing to follow a question to its answer and, likely, subsequent query. Yet, however far afield his inquiries led, Homer kept a close connection to a local story or common concern.

The reader will encounter footnotes throughout the text. These have all been added by us in an attempt to clarify references and to acknowledge the significance of relevant history. Homer often quotes literature, refers to prominent figures, or speaks about local folklore. Wanting to help readers have a robust encounter with his writings, we have provided additional context and citation, remaining aware that too much interruption can become burdensome. It should be noted that we could not find sources for all references, and as a result there may be an occasional omission of information where more is wanted. We sympathize with you and accept full responsibility for lapses and any errors we may have committed in this process.

There are times when the reader may see a phrase or description that does not accord with contemporary sensibilities. Some of Homer's sentiments are dated and certain of his usages are no longer in vogue. But these seem to have more to do with the mores of his era than with any underlying attitude or prejudice. Thus, when he encourages "ladies" to get out their "dough dishes," it reflects less of his feelings toward women than does his tribute to Mary Clarke or his consistent reference to his determined and resourceful spouse, Dees, for whom his affection and high regard are obvious throughout his writing. Likewise, his use of the term "Indian" to describe the many individuals he encountered among the Maliseet people of western New Brunswick reflects both the official and unofficial usage of his day. But his deep and abiding admiration and respect for Indigenous people consistently comes to the fore. Finally, the reader will note the occasional inclusion of words such as "I quote" or "end of quotation" by which Homer signalled to his audience that he was reading material from another source. We have retained these as a reminder of the format in which the essays were first delivered.

The Legacy

Ken Homer always seemed to have an apt quotation or literary or historical reference at hand for any occasion. His essays reflect this ability, and his frequent resort to fragments of original source material enhanced the experience of his listeners (and now, readers), adding to their own store of knowledge. His humble delivery and relaxed presentation contributed to the wide acclaim that his essays gained. Homer was surely well-educated, possessing keen insight with considerable powers of observation. But one of his great gifts was his capacity for common sense and folk wisdom.

Many readers will have known Ken Homer personally and will immediately recognize in these essays the pleasant and genial aspects of his personality. Some may only have heard his radio broadcasts, and for them, too, his friendly and casual nature will be evident. For those who are introduced to Homer here for the first time, his humility and grace shine through on the printed page as clearly as they did to all those he encountered in both his professional and avocational pursuits. Homer leaves no trace of condescension or intellectual showiness. Perhaps the greatest appeal of this book is that all readers may find something of interest and value in Homer's natural curiosity, his benevolent regard for nature, and his insightful understanding of the human condition.

We may liken him to Michel de Montaigne. This 16th century French writer is credited with inventing the essay as a literary form in which he was able to wander discursively through the myriad topics that captivated his mind without the necessity of thematic consistency or systematic organization. Montaigne was curious about himself and the world around him, and he cast a penetrating and thoughtful gaze on all of it.

Homer read Montaigne and clearly practiced his methods. But, whereas Montaigne wrote his essays in order to compose a kind of self-portrait, reflecting his moving mind and alive to his complexities, Homer instead seeks not his own image, but the world's. From his station in Upper Woodstock, he uses his pen, paper, and microphone to paint a portrait of the world he inhabits and the traditions that support it. Especially for readers who have lived in the areas he describes or within his shared heritage, Homer enlivens that world by giving it greater depth. He adds colour to the black and white images of the past.

Reading the essays aloud (which we recommend heartily) will put proof to Homer's prowess as a masterful storyteller.

Homer was an observer, training a keen eye on the natural world around him and on the habits and propensities of his fellow travellers, present and past. In the title essay of this volume, he remarks on what is discovered when one pauses to give the world more than the passing glance with which we are accustomed to regarding it. "I've often benefitted," he says, "from the knowledge that the investment of a few minutes' silent waiting yields many more of interesting observations." It is his attention to the seemingly ordinary that moves us. When Homer looks around his homestead along the river, drenched in "roseate light," he sees the "glittering landscape" and the coming night sky's "marshalling of the constellations." His curiosity pushes ours; his inquisitiveness is infectious. The gnarled roots of a tree, or the plaque of commemoration—now they cling to our view more tightly.

These essays invite us to be attentive to the moments of our lives, whether they be lively conversations with friends, the scurrying of the tiniest field mouse, or quiet times of solitude. Homer cares about the subjects of his writing and he recognizes their inherent value and importance as aspects of our shared lives. He is an ardent observer from his post on the St. John River valley, and he inspires us to care deeply for his subject matter, to feel the enrichment and satisfaction it occasions—not only vicariously through his writing, but personally, in a learned behaviour. We are called to make our attention habitual, to emulate his concern and replicate his dedicated curiosity. We must follow his example: "I learned to look for what there was to see."

What might we draw from our lives if we take this approach to each day?

Homer's writings show us how to engage with the world and people around us. With endless wonder and enthusiasm, the cosmos will open herself up to the inquisitive student; familiar people and locations will take on a new lustre; one will encounter the "life force" beating throughout the natural world; and, from time to time, we may glimpse the boundless "mysteries of life and growth."

Stuart Kinney & Ross Kinney

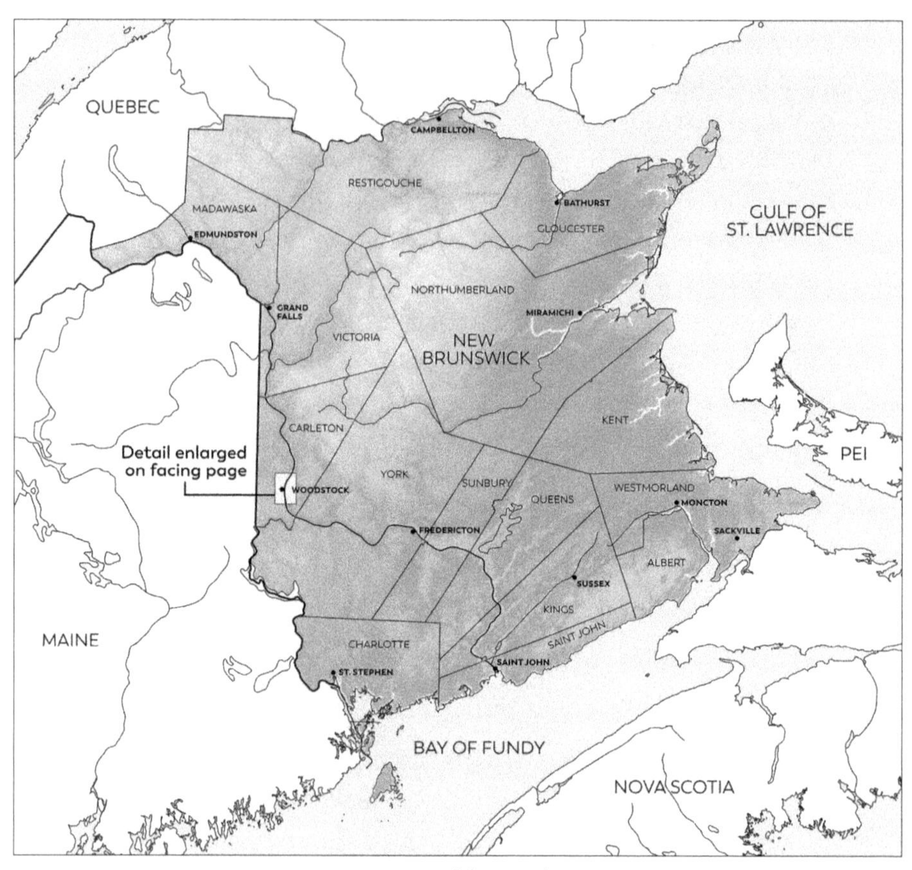

New Bruswick, Canada.

Woodstock Before the Dam

Woodstock and the surrounding area prior to the Mactaquac Dam

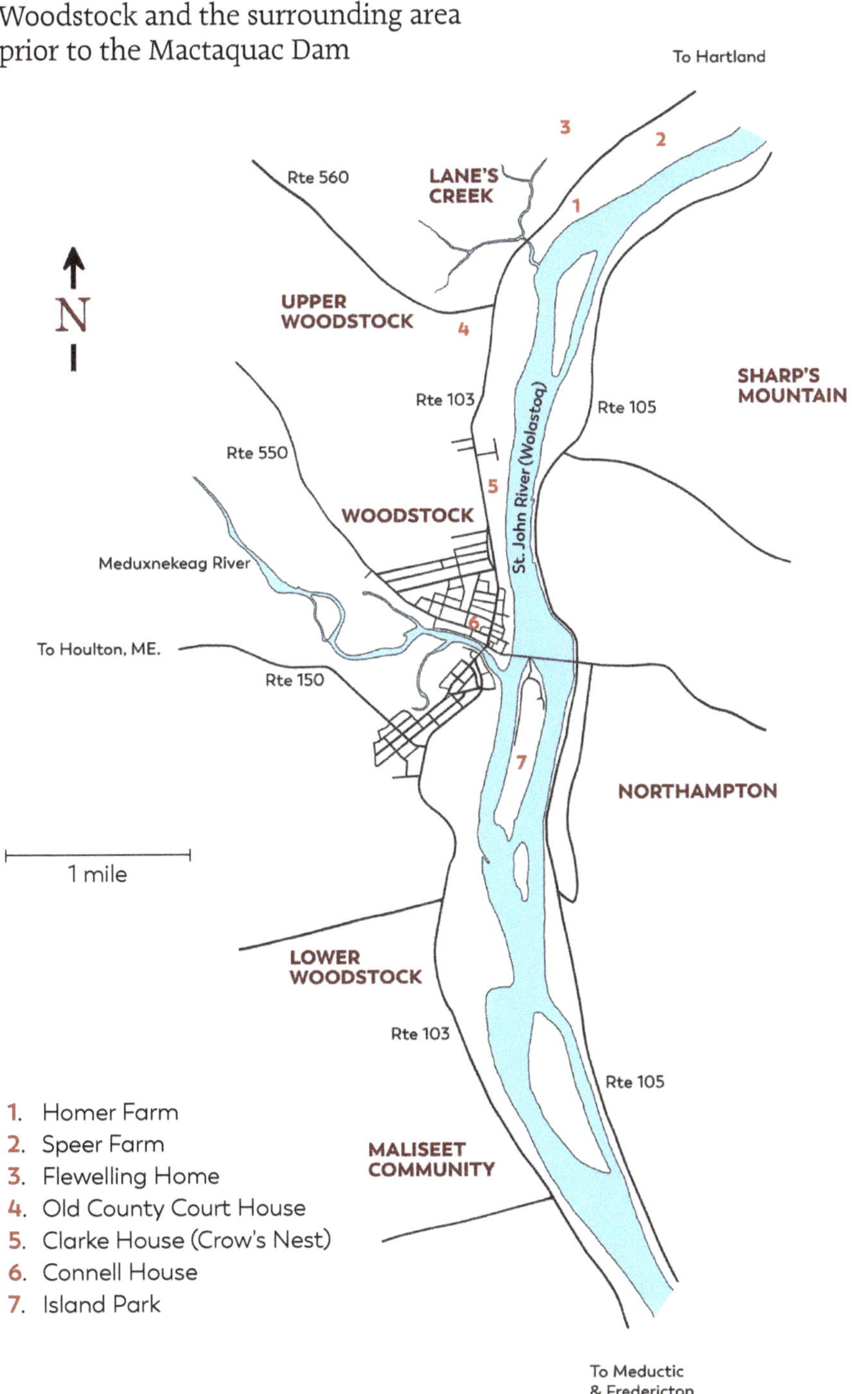

1. Homer Farm
2. Speer Farm
3. Flewelling Home
4. Old County Court House
5. Clarke House (Crow's Nest)
6. Connell House
7. Island Park

Ken Homer, August 1976. (Photo by Mary Bernard)

People & Places

This directory provides details for references to locations and contemporaries in the Homers' daily lives. Ken Homer shares his life in his essays, using the homestead, the townsfolk, and local institutions as subject matter. By providing brief descriptions, we hope to paint a clearer picture of his world in Upper Woodstock.

Dees Homer - (1919-2008) daughter of George Frederick and Mary Clarke. Mary Elizabeth Pedrick Clarke was Ken Homer's spouse for 64 years, and was the catalyst for the acquisition in 1945 of their farm in Upper Woodstock, a locus of the inspiration for so many of the essays. A passionate conservationist in her own right, she campaigned against the construction of the Mactaquac Dam. She was a founder of the Carleton County Historical Society and an instrumental figure in the meticulous restoration of the Old County Court House in Upper Woodstock.

Stephen Homer - son of Ken and Dees Homer. A biologist by training, he became a photographer and writer for magazines such as *Harrowsmith* and *Equinox* in the 1980s. For over 20 years, with the support of his wife Anne Durand, he operated a certified organic vegetable farm at Senneville on Montreal's West Island where they have been proponents of community-supported agriculture. From 2014-18 they also operated a cafe in Montreal.

George Frederick Clarke - (1883-1974) Homer's father-in-law. A dentist by trade and author, archaeologist, and salmon angler by avocation, Clarke was renowned for his writing and enjoyed the company of many famous Canadian literary figures such as Bliss Carman and Charles G.D. Roberts. His influence on Homer was profound and his home on Main St. in Woodstock was the location of many memorable gatherings.

Mary Clarke – (1889-1995) wife of George Frederick Clarke. Born in Philadelphia, Mary Schubert first met Clarke during his studies in dentistry there in 1910. They wed in 1912 and settled in Woodstock where their two daughters, Dees and Jane, were born. Mary was active in the social life of the town and devoted to her family. She presided over the hospitality of the Clarke house and saw the comings and goings of family, friends and visitors over many decades. Following the death of her husband in 1974, she remained the matriarch at the Clarke house.

Aunty Ruby Clarke – (1892 - 1979) younger sister to George Frederick Clark. After her fiancé died in WWI, she never married and suffered from ill health through much of her life. She was a regular in the Clarke house during her brother's lifetime and continuing through the period when Ken and Dees Homer resided there as well.

Dr. Peter Paul – (1902-89) an elder of the Maliseet community located near Woodstock. Paul was a friend to George Frederick Clarke and Ken Homer, and a frequent visitor in both their homes. Recognized for his contributions to the preservation of Maliseet language and culture, he was awarded a Doctor of Letters by the University of New Brunswick in 1970 and was inducted into the Order of Canada in 1987. Homer chronicled his life in an extensive autobiographical audio interview now housed in the Provincial Archives of New Brunswick.

Tappan Adney – (1868-1950) husband of Minnie Bell Sharp, friend of George Frederick Clarke and Peter Paul. Born in Ohio and university educated by age 15, Adney first travelled to Upper Woodstock in 1887 at the invitation of Minnie Bell Sharp (daughter of Francis Peabody Sharp), whom he met in New York City where she had come to study music and had taken lodgings at his mother's boarding house. The visit to New Brunswick altered the course of his life. His encounter with the wilderness environment, and especially with the Maliseet people, inspired his work as writer, artist, ethnologist, and conservator of Indigenous culture, especially the knowledge of how to build birch bark canoes.

Bill Turney – close friend to Ken and Dees Homer. Born in Fredericton, NB, and educated in music at Mount Allison University and the University of Toronto, he served as music teacher at Woodstock High School in the 1960s, and then at Ricker College in Houlton, Maine. He was the choir director at St. Luke's Anglican Church in Woodstock. Turney was also active as a leader in Boy Scouts and with Canada's centennial Young Voyageur program. He served as president of the New Brunswick Youth Orchestra in the 1970s.

David Bell – a frequent visitor to the Homer household. Born in Woodstock, Bell has served as a member of the University of New Brunswick faculty since 1985, teaching both Law and History. He has written extensively on New Brunswick Loyalist history and on local subjects such as music teacher Minnie Bell Sharp, and the prosecution of Dr. Peter Paul in 1946 for harvesting black ash, in the exercise of his Indigenous right, on privately held woodland.

The Speers – next-door neighbours to the Homers at Upper Woodstock. Robert Joseph Speer, his wife Alma, and their two children Robert John and Jane lived on a dairy farm north of Homers on the same intervale. The elder Robert was named as godfather to Stephen Homer and the two children were like siblings to him, sharing farm chores as well as various childhood adventures and explorations. The Speer family descended from the Irish immigrants who first settled Speerville, NB, southwest of Woodstock, in the mid-1800s.

Lillian Flewelling – (1924-96) neighbour to the Homers at Upper Woodstock. Husband Nelson and Lillian and their four children Linda, Terry, Glen, and Chris, occupied the adjacent farm just north of the Homer property on Rte 103. Lillian worked as a housekeeper for Mrs. Clarke and, eventually, when age and infirmity took its toll on Dees, she performed similar duties for her as well.

The Homer Farm – an acreage on the bank of the St. John River at Upper Woodstock. Accessed by a meandering dirt lane off Rte 103 above Lane's Creek, the farm was acquired by Ken and Dees Homer in 1945. It served as the focal point of their life, and his writing, from the 1950s until the early '70s when the house was destroyed by spring ice jams. This damage resulted from the construction of the Mactaquac Dam in 1968 and the associated flooding of the intervale where the farmhouse was located.

The Clarke House – the residence of George Frederick and Mary Clarke on Main St. in Woodstock, NB. Built in 1905 by surveyor Charles Garden, the two-storey Regency-style brick residence was known as "Crow's Nest" after the famous railway pass in the Canadian Rockies which Garden helped to survey. It was acquired by the Clarkes in 1913 and served as their home for the remainder of their lives. Centered on a large, well-treed lot, the house has a notable symmetry in its exterior aspects and interior layout. It was designated as a New Brunswick Provincial Historic Site in 1978. Homer and his wife Dees occupied the house as their principal residence following the destruction of their Upper Woodstock farmhouse.

Shieldy – the titular three-legged cat, named by Stephen Homer for a distinctive marking on her forehead. The farm in Upper Woodstock where she was born was home to many animals, including cats, dogs, a rabbit, and occasionally an injured wild bird. The Homers' fondness for these companions is evident throughout the essays as Scamper, the cat, and Princess, the dog, play their roles in the stories being told. When Shieldy died in 1981 at the advanced age of 18 years, she was buried among the flowers on the hillside overlooking the farm. Homer penned a touching eulogy, reflecting on her attachment to their home and her capacity for stimulating his own appreciation for the natural world, concluding: "She will always hold a place of prominence among the animal shades that dwell in the memories of our family life."

Sharp's Mountain – a high hill in the Parish of Northampton. Situated on the east side of the St. John River opposite Upper Woodstock, its name arises from its location on or near lands originally granted by the Crown in 1796 to Alexander Sharp, grandfather to the renowned horticulturist Francis Peabody Sharp.

Lane's Creek - a small creek flowing into the St. John River at Upper Woodstock. Draining a large area of Woodstock and Wakefield parishes, it flows into the river just below the entrance to the Homer property on lands originally granted to Ephraim Lane. In 1848, Woodstock Iron Works constructed a blast furnace at the creek's mouth to smelt the high-quality ore located nearby in Upper Woodstock and Jacksonville. In 1887, following his arrival from New York, Tappan Adney first encountered local Maliseet Peter Joe at Lane's Creek, where he saw him building a birch bark canoe.

Mactaquac Dam - hydroelectric dam constructed on the St. John River in the 1960s near Kingsclear, NB. When it was completed in 1968, the dam created a headpond which flooded an area that stretched nearly to Hartland, NB, submerging countless islands, the rich agricultural lands of the intervale flats (including the site of the Homer farm), Indigenous sites, graveyards and other historic properties. It was an integral component of a system of hydroelectric generation stations designed and implemented by the New Brunswick Electric Power Commission to address long-term energy needs for the province. Nevertheless, it was opposed vigorously by a vocal group of citizens, including George Frederick Clarke and Ken and Dees Homer, who called themselves The Association for the Preservation and Development of the St. John River in its Natural State.

Carleton County Historical Society - the brainchild of the Homers, organized in 1960. Its original mission was the acquisition and restoration of the Old County Court House in Upper Woodstock, but it also acquired numerous other historic properties in the area, including Connell House, the home of the famous New Brunswick Postmaster Charles Connell, now a National Historic Site. The Homers were the driving force behind the Society for more than two decades — Ken serving as president as well as organizer and cook at the annual salmon fry fundraiser, while Dees provided indomitable energy and unwavering insistence on historically accurate restoration work.

Walks With A Three-Legged Cat

Winter

Molasses

1981

The other day we were having lunch at the Clarke house — some delicious homemade chicken soup. Our friend Lillian Flewelling was there and she happened to mention that when she was a little girl and came home from school for lunch to find that her mother had made soup, she was unhappy that day because she didn't like soup. I asked her what she would have for lunch instead and she said she'd usually have bread and molasses.

That started us off briefly on the subject of molasses, and Lillian pointed out that in the old days in country kitchens a pitcher of molasses was as much a fixture on the table at meal time as butter or salt and pepper. It was used as a spread or on buckwheat pancakes in the absence of maple honey. Some people poured extra molasses over their home baked beans. Molasses cakes and cookies and puddings were favoured foods, and a molasses taffy pull was often a social occasion.

Certainly the molasses jug, along with the vinegar jug and the jug for kerosene to fill the lamps, made frequent trips to the grocery store where it was replenished from the spigot on the big wooden cask. I remembered the term "blackstrap molasses" as being a dietary fad a few years ago about the time that yogurt became popular and wondered why it was called that. After lunch I went to look it up.

Among the meanings for "blackstrap" were: "a common red wine of the Mediterranean" and "a drink consisting of rum and molasses." Perhaps blackstrap molasses, then, would be the kind used to make the drink known as blackstrap. In any case, blackstrap molasses is what is left after all the sugar possible has been crystallized out of sugarcane or sugar beet juice.

I discovered that sugarcane has been known and used since prehistoric times. It's thought to have originated in New Guinea from where it was transported to southeast Asia. The first written reference is to sugarcane grown in Northern India in the 4th century BC. The word sugar derives from the Sanskrit *sharkera*. The Sanskrit for solidified sugar is *khanda* and that's where we get the word "candy."

Arabs spread the culture of sugarcane through northern Africa and southern Europe and the Chinese, who introduced methods of extracting sugar from the cane, carried it to Java and the Philippines. Commercial manufacture developed in Egypt in the 9th and 10th centuries. At first sugar was a scarce luxury dispersed by apothecaries and often used for medicinal purposes. Later, especially after the introduction of sugar cane to the New World, large supplies became available. Columbus carried sugar cane to Santa Domingo on his second voyage in 1493, and Cortés, Pizarro, and other explorers took cane to the mainland of Central and South America. By 1600, raw sugar production in tropical America was the largest industry in the world of that day.

Beets, on the other hand, have been used for sugar production for less than two centuries though they now yield about 40 percent of the world's supply. The first factory was built in Silesia in 1803. Napoleon encouraged beet sugar production in France during the blockade days of the French wars. The abolition of slavery in the West Indies in 1843 resulted in a great spurt of European sugar beet production.

But to get back to molasses: the word is a Portuguese derivation from a Latin word meaning "as sweet as honey." Molasses, as has been said, is a by-product of raw sugar production whereas what the English call treacle is a product of the refining process. The word "treacle" underlines the early medicinal use of sugar and sugar products since it is derived from a Greek word meaning an antidote for poisonous bites. The Dormouse at the Mad Tea Party in *Alice in Wonderland* was not as far out as he seemed when he told the story of the three little girls who lived in a treacle well because of the medicinal properties of their water.

Until 1943, the chief commercial use for molasses was fermentation to produce industrial ethyl alcohol and rum. When production of alcohol from ethylene decreased the market for fermentation alcohol there was a marked lowering in the price of molasses and it became more attractive as a feed for farm animals — and that's where most molasses goes today. If urea and other non-protein nitrogen is added to fed molasses then microorganisms in the rumens of cattle can synthesize their own protein from these sources.

Well, I may not be too sure of the origin of the word "blackstrap" but I did learn a lot I hadn't known about molasses, all because there was once a little girl who didn't like soup for lunch.

The Exploits Of Gabe Acquin

1982

Last Saturday afternoon our friend Dr. Peter Paul dropped in for a cup of tea and, as often happens when Peter comes to call, he brought with him something he thought we'd be interested in seeing. This time it was a black coiled notebook about six inches long and four wide inscribed on the cover as follows:

> Diplomatic and State Correspondence of the Milicite Indian Gabe[1] — together with a record of visitations and levees held by the chief during the first International Fisheries Exhibition of 1883.

Inside the covers were pages on which had been pasted some three dozen calling cards, many of them from former British officers who had known Gabe Acquin during their overseas service in New Brunswick some 20 years before. There were many blank pages in the notebook from which former contents had been removed and it makes you wonder what signatures might have been appended to the missing correspondence.

Austin Squires, in his history of Fredericton,[2] refers to Gabe as "the most renowned of the Malicites during the 19th century" and speaks of the special relationships some of the Indians had with the lieutenant-governors and garrison officers who loved to spend their leisure time on hunting and fishing expeditions. When the Prince of

1 Gabe Acquin (c.1811-1901) prominent Wolastoq'kew guide, hunter, and interpreter who often accompanied British officers stationed in Fredericton on hunting trips. He is recognized as an emissary and statesman of his people and by the St. Mary's First Nation as their founder.

2 Dr. William Austin Squires (1905-1978), wrote *A History of Fredericton — The Last 200 Years* (republished in 1980).

Wales, later to become Edward VII, visited Fredericton in 1860,[3] it was Gabe who took the Prince for a canoe ride on the St. John River from behind Government House to the mouth of the Nashwaaksis, much to the distress of officialdom and to the delight of the young visitor. And Gabe accompanied Lt.-Gov. Arthur Hamilton-Gordon on his wilderness journeys of 1862-63.[4]

In 1883, when the first International Fisheries Exhibition was held in England, Gabe was sent to London as part of the Canadian exhibit. He set up his wigwam at South Kensington and he had a birchbark canoe on the artificial lakes there. Many of the officers who had known him in Fredericton entertained their old guide in their London clubs and invited him to their country homes. This was the first of two visits Gabe made to London and Dr. Squires records that "on both occasions he proved an extraordinarily fine ambassador of his native land."

Only one sample of correspondence survives in the notebook — letters from Capt. George H. Best of Bournemouth inviting Gabe to come for a visit. One, dated 10th July 1883, reads in part:

> My dear Gabe,
>
> I have just heard from my brother that you are in London and that he has seen and spoken with you. I wish you would come down here and see me before you leave England. Write and tell me you will not leave England without seeing me. If you cannot come here, I shall see you in London and have a talk about old times — the best times I ever had and which I wish could come again.

Gabe evidently did accept the invitation because another letter dated September 13, 1883 concerns travel arrangements and Capt. Best states, "I wish you would bring your canoe as the weather seems likely

---

3 For the first Royal Visit in 60 years, Albert Edward, Prince of Wales, toured Upper and Lower Canada for two months. He visited Saint John, and in Fredericton he opened a "pleasure ground," what is now known as Wilmot Park.

4 *Wilderness Journeys in New Brunswick*, 1864.

to be fine and we could go out on to the river near here and show the natives what canoeing ought to be, but you must do as you like about it, I shall be glad to see you either with or without your canoe."

This seemed to be a typical reaction to the presence of Gabe in London as a living symbol of 20 year-old memories of wilderness experiences in New Brunswick. The same delight is evidenced in the printed words of those who wrote and had published descriptions of such experiences. Richard Dashwood, for example, in his *Chiploquorgan or Life by the Camp Fire in the Dominion of Canada & Newfoundland*,[5] in describing a January hunting trip, speaks of the delight of getting to camp after a fatiguing day, having a good meal and then a pipe filled with fragrant honey dew mixed with willow bark. And he says, "The perfect repose and comfort of that smoke cannot be described, nor would I, on such an occasion, exchange my situation for the best room in England, and the most cunningly designed arm chair ever produced." He adds, "Gabe proved a most amusing companion in camp, sang capital songs and told excellent hunting stories."

Governor Gordon, describing his periods of escape to the woods, very realistically recounts the disadvantages and difficulties of dealing with mosquitoes and sand fleas; but when he describes the advantages and the pleasures of wilderness life, he waxes almost lyrical and he writes:

> I have passed the night shivering on a mountainside, waiting for the dawn. I have passed it stretched on the long grass snatching short slumbers under the Syrian moonlight with my horse's bridle around my arms. I have spent it in many different places, under circumstances calculated to inspire strange and solemn thoughts, but never anywhere with so awful a sense of man's insignificance, and of the calm changelessness of nature, as in the depths of the North American forest.

---

5 Richard Lewes Dashwood (d.1905), British Army officer who enjoyed hunting and fishing. He travelled the major New Brunswick rivers on his way to Gaspé, Nova Scotia, and Newfoundland. *Chiploquorgan* (1871) was republished in 1979.

This kind of response to a feature of provincial life which most 19th century New Brunswickers simply took for granted helps to explain why Gabe Acquin received such a warm welcome on his visits to London, and why there are so many impressive calling cards in the little black notebook Peter Paul brought for us to look at and speculate about over a cup of tea.

Mincemeat

1980

Snow has fallen and the appearance of a white world, even if it's only temporary, arouses thoughts of the coming Christmas season. In country kitchens, preparations for the festive board have already begun with the gathering of ingredients for plum puddings, light fruit cakes, dark fruit cakes, and other traditional edibles. In many cases, these ingredients have already been subjected to the alchemy which transmutes them into prized objects of individual family tradition now carefully stored for curing against the coming of the joyous time. One of the important items in all this work of preparation is the making of the winter's mincemeat.

Recently my wife pointed out to me an interesting article on homemade mincemeat which appeared in the December '79 issue of *Early American Life*. The author, Martha Thomas, traced the history of mincemeat back to the days of an ancient Roman chef Apicius who wrote the first known cookbook and included recipes for preserving meat by the addition of honey. The idea became general in European countries where custodians of the kitchen discovered that sugar and spices would retard meat spoilage. This was the origin of the filling which, with the addition of apples and raisins and other items, was surrounded by pastry to give us mincemeat pie.

In Merrie England during the time of Good Queen Bess, the first Elizabeth, it was the custom to keep huge mincemeat pies on family tables during the 12 days of Christmas for the benefit of visitors who believed that there would be a happy month in the New Year for every day they tasted Christmas pie.

One of the things in Martha Thomas's article that I found of interest was her retelling of the story behind the nursery rhyme:

Little Jack Horner sat in a corner
Eating a Christmas pie,
He put in his thumb and pulled out a plum
And said, "What a good boy am I."

She says that when he put in his thumb and pulled out a plum he was really getting a raisin and that these were highly valued as additions to mincemeat and were used sparingly because they were rare and costly.

The nursery rhyme was recorded in Somerset in 1725 and local tradition has it that the Jack Horner of the rhyme was in fact a certain Thomas Horner of Mells who did well for himself during the dissolution of the monasteries. According to Martha Thomas's version, Horner was a steward to Richard Whiting, a wealthy abbot of Glastonbury Cathedral during the reign of Henry VIII. The plump prelate incurred the King's wrath because of his personal excesses, particularly in association with food. He finally felt the full force of the King's fury when he built a grand kitchen equipped with every convenience. To appease the King, Whiting dispatched Horner with the gift of a great mincemeat pie. The steward lifted up the top crust to see what had been concocted to tease the appetite of the King and found not only mincemeat, but the deeds to 12 different estates. The temptation was too great. "How will the King know," he thought as he helped himself to one of the deeds. "Besides, possession is nine-tenths of the law." He delivered the pie to King Henry and took up residence as a country squire. The ensuing rhyme gave us the word "plum" as a description of an important political award.

Mince pies found favour in North America and have certainly become part of the Christmas tradition of many Canadian families along with other adjuncts of the Charles Dickens kind of Victorian Christmas. I remember a sentence from an article that appeared in a mid-1860s issue of a magazine entitled *The Leisure Hour*. It was entitled "The Christmas Face of London" or something like that, and the sentence I remember is: "There goes a family of laughing children to dine with grandmamma who has plum-puddinged and roast-goosed and mince-pied and Christmas-treed every one of them every year since they knew what Christmas was."

All this talk of pies reminds me of the story about the old lady who was a great baker and every Thursday her oven was kept busy from very early in the morning. Shortly after noon a friend came in and was admiring the numerous pies placed in various places about the kitchen, all fork-marked with the letters "TM."

"What do the letters mean?" asked the friend.

"Oh, I like to mark all my pies so I can tell them apart. The TM on these here means 'Tis Mince."

"But what about those over there?"

"Oh," said the old lady, "Those over there are apple, so naturally the TM means 'Tain't Mince."

The Christmas Tree

1979

Our late Aunty Ruby was a great one for collecting memorabilia and making notes about things that interested and amused her. Among these was a brief description of the time when our son Stephen, who was then a university student, came home from a foray into the wilds of Carleton County with a particularly memorable Christmas tree. It was so wide and so thick that as it was carried toward the house you couldn't see the young man behind it. "It seemed," recorded Aunty Ruby's note, "as though the tree were coming along all by itself. And Ken said, 'It looked like Birnam Wood coming to Dunsinane.'"

That was indeed a magnificent tree, standing in the living room of our old farmhouse, tinsel and baubles glittering in light from the fireplace — and I remember it well as I remember many another tree now in the care and keeping of the Spirit of Christmas Past.

There were the trees of my childhood home in Yarmouth — star-topped and hung with trimmings that included Victorian angels — the last thing we saw before bedtime on Christmas Eve and the first thing that met our eyes when my sister and my two brothers and I raced down the stairs very early on Christmas morning. There were the trees of the years we all went to grandfather's house for Christmas dinner. We didn't have to go over the river and through the woods to get there but sometimes, when I was very young and there was snow enough, a one-horse sleigh was sent to pick us up, with bells jingling, horses' hooves clopping, a warm buffalo robe around us, and the whispering sound of the metal runners on the hard-packed snow. The tree was in a corner of the south parlour near the Franklin stove, standing guard over the gifts until dinner was over and all the uncles and aunts and cousins crowded in, and Aunt Hilda ceremoniously dispensed the presents.

There were the trees in the firelit living room of my late father-in-law Dr. G.F. Clarke in Woodstock, and memory draws him for me now, sitting in the big wing chair by the fireplace, smoke rising from the bowl of the pipe clenched firmly in his teeth, his eyes twinkling with the pleasure of having his family 'round him on Christmas night.

The Clarke Christmas trees have been rather unusual in that for the past two decades they have done double duty. It has become traditional for Dr. Peter Paul to choose and supply a tree for the annual Christmas meeting of the Carleton County Historical Society, and after the meeting is over the tree is taken to the Clarke house to be set up again at the proper time. Over the years, on a night before the Society meeting, there has always been a gathering of members to string the popcorn and cranberries that deck the boughs in traditional fashion — and there have always been two or more young people among the stringers. The sound of young voices plays a dominant role in the musical portion of the evening and one of the songs that is always included in the program is about a Christmas tree. The song was composed by Col. W.T. Baird, author of *70 Years of New Brunswick Life*,[6] with music by W.O. Perkins, and it was written especially for a Christmas party at Col. Baird's home, Willowell, on Dec. 26th, 1890, when it was sung by four of his granddaughters all about 14 years of age.

In 1965 I was present when Bill Turney was energetically rehearsing with the group of girls who would be singing at the Society meeting that year a version of the Willowell song:

> Here again we're glad to meet you,
> Under rooftree gathered 'round.
> Where the bells ring out a welcome,
> 'Tis to us a joyful sound.
>
> So let the time fly fast as it may,
> We'll be happy on Christmas Day,
> Members of one family,
> Gathered 'round our Christmas tree.

---

6 William T. Baird (1819-1897) lived much of his life in and around Woodstock. He was a prominent military man, while also active as a pharmacist, librarian, and author. *70 Years of New Brunswick Life* (1890) was republished in 1978.

From England's isles and Scotia's borders,
Here we are formed in one band.
At Willowell we're glad to meet you,
Fairest spot in all the land.

So let the time fly fast as it may,
We'll be happy on Christmas Day,
Members of one family,
Gathered 'round our Christmas tree.

As you gather with your families 'round the tree this Christmastide, may I wish you all a very merry Christmas.

A Clarke House Christmas Dinner

1980

Christmas is almost here and there has been less opportunity than usual to enjoy the seasonal signs in the world of nature. But one afternoon recently the sun showed itself for long enough to set the late December world agleam with pre-holiday splendour, and at its setting the hills across the river were suffused with the roseate light one looks forward to at Christmas time. Earlier that afternoon as I was admiring the glittering landscape, I heard a flutter of wings and 'round the house came half a dozen rose-breasted grosbeaks, their plumage stained with colour much like December sunsets, and a moment later they were joined by six evening grosbeaks adding their white and black and gold to the sunlit winter scene.

There was one clear night recently, crackling with sub-zero cold, when there was a rare chance to notice the marshalling of the constellations towards their Christmas stations. The December half moon marked the snow with long shadows as I found Cassiopaea's chair directly overhead, Orion striding above the eastern hill across the river in his perennial pursuit of the Seven Sisters, and the Big Dipper with a Christmastime tilt on its handle above the northern hill.

At the G.F. Clarke house in Woodstock, preparations for Christmas Day are in full spate. The kitchen has been the source of delicious odours and the bake oven, like a cornucopia, has been supplying such items as the plum puddings carefully stored in the traditional toffee tin, and the currant cake in the crock with the deluxe white fruit cake. And there's Mrs. Clarke's special pineapple cake and Dees's chocolate chip cookies and I don't know what else. There are ruby-coloured bottles of prepared cranberries in the cold room and the turkey lies awaiting in the shed. Our friend Lillian Flewelling has been polishing the sideboard silver with gusto and the decorations have been moved within easy reach. Already the wreaths are at the many-paned front windows and above the door knocker, and the tree is on its base in the garage out of reach of the whirling snow.

Having married into Christmas dinners at the Clarke house over four decades ago now, I am the fortunate possessor of many enjoyable memories of the days when Dr. Clarke and Aunty Ruby were still with us. I can see him now standing before the huge golden brown turkey on the table, lifting the gleaming carving knife from its elegant cut glass rest, making a tentative move or two with it and then saying, "Take this damn thing away and bring me something that will cut," and Dees or her sister Jane had to fetch a sharp kitchen knife before he would proceed.

I can see our Stephen as a young lad watching wide-eyed and listening intently to the dinner table exchange of amusing stories by his elders about the old days and old ways or Aunty Ruby's comments on Bertie Boyer's wry statements concerning many aspects of life. Dr. Clarke would generally step in and pre-empt any controversial subject and lest his eloquent summation of it offend one or the other of its originators, Mum Clarke would dispose of it directly with her "now Fred, it's time to talk about something else."

And there was much talk and laughter, especially hearty when Jane's antic humour held sway, until finally Dr. Clarke, more often than not in later years, would excuse himself with courtly politeness and retreat to the living room and sit in the big chair by the fire where much of his writing had been done, and smoke his pipe in peaceful solitude until the table was cleared and the whole assemblage descended upon him again for the exchange of the family presents from under the Christmas tree.

This year, the old traditions will play their wonted role. All the leaves will be needed in the long table as 13 or 14 of us will gather 'round it in the panelled dining room, including three of Mrs. Clarke's great-grandchildren who now in their turn will sit wide-eyed admiring the roses in the centre of the table and the candles and the gleaming silver and china against the white linen cloth and the glass goblets with their cranberry trim, and they'll be listening to adult reminiscences and laughing at the antics of their grandmother Jane. And all of us will be pleased that the president of the cheerful proceedings will still be the gracious lady with soft waved silver hair and wide blue eyes alert to see that all is going well in the current celebration of her 91st Christmas.

The holiday will have come and gone before you hear from me again on this program so may I now wish you one and all a very Merry Christmas.

First Loyalist Winter In Fredericton

1976

One day not long ago when the great cold had come down from the north with strong winds to reinforce it, I had occasion to walk for about a mile in the bitter weather. There is something frightening about intense cold. We don't ordinarily recognize this because in the present day and age we have means to mitigate it or avoid it altogether. But as I walked briskly along with the wind's fingers pinching my cheeks and my nostrils narrowing with each intake of frigid air, I wondered how I would feel without the surety of welcoming warmth at the end of that brief journey.

New Brunswick's first historian, Peter Fisher,[7] tells us about the hardships of the first Loyalist founders of Fredericton who experienced a cold winter that began much like this one. Many of the members of the Provincial Regiments who had been granted land on the upper St. John River elected to remain at the port for the winter, but others moved up in small boats despite the lateness of the season. To quote Mr. Fisher:

> Scarcely had they begun to construct their cabins, when they were surprised by the rigours of an untried climate, their habitations being enveloped in snow before they were tenantable. The privations and suffering of some of these people almost exceed belief. Frequently in the piercing cold of winter, a part of the family had to

7 Peter Fisher (1782-1848), an early Loyalist historian. He is the father of Lewis Peter, mayor of Woodstock; Charles, a Father of Confederation; Anne, wife of Charles Connell; and grandfather to Annie Connell Fisher, who married George Robert Parkin, headmaster of Fredericton Collegiate School where Bliss Carman and Charles G.D. Roberts came under his tutelage. Annie and George were grandparents to philosopher George Grant, and their daughter married Vincent Massey, the first Canadian-born governor general. A family of deep Loyalist tradition.

> remain up during the night to keep fire in their huts to prevent the other part (of the family) from freezing. Some very destitute families made use of boards to supply the want of bedding; the father or some of the elder children remaining up by turns and warming two suitable pieces of boards, which they applied alternately to the smaller children to keep them warm, with many similar expedients.[8]

And W.O. Raymond, historian of the St. John River, has this to add:

> The awfulness of the situation may be readily imagined. Women, delicately reared, cared for their infants beneath canvas tents, rendered habitable only by the banks of snow which lay six feet deep in the open spaces of the forest. Men unaccustomed to toil looked with dismay at the prospect before them. The non-arrival of supplies expected before the close of navigation added much to their distress. At one time starvation stared them in the face, and, as one who passed through the sorrowful experience of that time has said, 'strong proud men cried like children, and, exhausted by cold and famine, lay down in their snow bound tents to die.' These poor settlers had to make frequent trips of from 50 to 100 miles with hand-sleds or toboggans through pathless woods and on the ice, to procure a precarious supply of food for their famishing families.
>
> Mrs. Lodewick Fisher used to relate to her grandchildren that soon after the arrival of the regiments at St. John, her family joined a party bound up the river in a schooner to St. Anne's (today's Fredericton).... On the 8th of October they reached their destination, and pitched their tents at Salamanca near the shore. Before any effectual steps had been taken to provide a shelter, winter was at hand.

8 *Sketches of New Brunswick*, 1825. The author's grandson republished the text in 1921 as *The First History of New Brunswick*.

> Snow fell on the 2nd of November to a depth of six inches. The best that some of the unfortunate people could do was to pitch their tents in the depths of the forest. Stones formed their rude fireplace. The tent had no floor but the ground. The winter was cold but the deep snow afforded some protection. Still it was an awful winter. There were mothers who had been reared in a pleasant country, enjoying the luxuries of life, who now clasped their helpless little ones to their bosoms and tried by the warmth of their own bodies to protect them from the bitter cold.
>
> Many of the weaker ones died from cold and exposure. Graves were dug with axes and shovels nearby, and there in stormy weather, the survivors laid their loved ones without any religious service for they had no clergyman.[9]

As I have said, there is something frightening about intense cold.

9 W.O. Raymond (1853-1923), clergyman and Loyalist historian from Woodstock. *Glimpses of the Past. History of the River St. John A.D. 1604-1784.* Saint John, 1905. Mrs. Lodewick Fisher was the mother of Peter Fisher. "Lodewick" was a variant of her husband's name which was "Lewis."

Sick With A Cold

1980

For several days this week I have shared the unhappy fate of those thousands of unfortunate individuals who are playing host to viruses or bacteria or germs or whatever, as the young people say. As always, it is a humbling, frustrating, and unpleasant experience.

When I do come down with a cold, it so often happens after a brief period of feeling extra well and full of energy that I sometimes wonder whether the switch to misery isn't the result of hubris, the name the ancient Greek tragedians gave to the self-congratulating smugness which rouses the anger of the gods. On the other hand, if you approach the question scientifically, perhaps the deceptive healthy condition arises from the fact that your body is busy marshalling its defences against an enemy already invading the citadel without your conscious knowledge.

This is the kind of aimless speculation that goes on in the mind as one lies there, head plugged, throat sore, chest constricted, feeling sorry for oneself and slipping in and out of a comatose state that isn't as satisfactory as real sleep because it seems impossible to put the mind to rest. And this kind of virus-infected, medication-influenced thought can fool you. The other night my racing mind seemed to me to be performing so well that its thoughts appeared most significant and I kept telling myself that I must be sure to remember them in the morning. But, alas, when morning came, memory had little of value to offer me.

It reminded me of the story of English author Thomas deQuincey[10] who was certain that under the influence of drugs he conceived literary masterpieces. So the next time he indulged, he made sure there were pen and paper handy. When he felt himself to be properly inspired

10 (1785-1859) English essayist and critic, and author of *Confessions of an English Opium-Eater.*

he seized the pen and wrote rapidly before drifting off to sleep. In the morning he eagerly seized the paper only to find some meaningless scratches and one shaky sentence which read, "There is a strong smell of turpentine over all."

One of the problems in being in bed with a cold is that you can't seem to concentrate on anything except feeling miserable for very long. You take up the book you have been waiting impatiently to read, but after a few pages you put it aside. You do find though, that there is a tendency to try to break the monotony of the passing moments by letting your eyes linger longer than usual on objects in the room about you. I happened to be in the spoolbed in the den in my mother-in-law's house and there were some interesting objects there. I looked over at the piece of furniture with its three drawers in the base, a turn-down writing desk board with smaller drawers behind it and three bookshelves behind glassed doors above it. It is believed that that little desketcetera might have belonged to Judith Morehouse and the sight of it set me thinking again of the story of Judith Jenkins Smith Morehouse and of how she was responsible for much property in Woodstock getting tied up in 999 year leases.[11]

Above the fireplace mantel is a 1960 Tom Forestall painting of the inn in Fredericton, built by one of my late father-in-law's ancestors and site of the first meeting of the New Brunswick legislature upon its removal to the capital of the new province. It was demolished to clear part of the site for the building of the Beaverbrook Theatre and I remembered the controversy over the examining architect's pronouncement that the old historic landmark was too much infested with dry rot to be saved in any case. The beams had looked pretty sound to me as I watched the inn come down. A couple of paintings

---

11 Judith (Jenkins) Smith Morehouse (c.1787-1857), the daughter of a Loyalist who served in the Revolutionary War, and the wife of Richard Smith, the eldest son of Captain Jacob Smith of 1st de Lancey's Brigade. Jacob was one of the first settlers in the area which was to become the town of Woodstock, and he and Richard would build some of the earliest known houses along the Meduxnekeag River. Judith eventually inherited this land, which, due to a proviso in her husband's will, she decided to lease to tenants for a period of 999 years.

by Tappan Adney set me off on mental journeys all the way to the gold fields of the trail of '98[12] and back again, and other distractions also helped to pass the erratically moving time.

Let me extend my sympathy to all those who are fellow victims of viruses this week, as well as a friendly warning to accept your fate and wait it out. The common tendency to try to get back into action too soon could result in your having to start the whole miserable business all over again.

---

12 As a young photojournalist, Adney was sent to cover the Yukon gold rush for *Harper's Weekly* in 1897-98. His subsequent book, *The Klondike Stampede*, was one of many to chronicle this extraordinary event.

The Visible Wind

1982

As long as I can remember there has never before been a winter when I have heard so much talk about the wind. The long continuance of record cold in the mid-west and along the eastern seaboard of North America may have had something to do with it, providing opportunities for a winter counterpart to the summer saying, "It isn't the heat, it's the humidity." Now they say, "It isn't the cold, it's the wind." Much time and attention has been given in conversations and by the media to the "wind chill factor," whether it's measured in degree equivalents or measured in watts-per-whatever. The words "wind warning" in a weather forecast cause more people than usual to prick up their ears and worry about possible frostbite or power failure.

No one is supposed ever to have seen the wind but this is a truism that is often ignored. When you hear a roaring on a wooded hillside and watch the conifers nodding and bending back and forth, and the bare branches of the deciduous varieties gesticulating wildly, what you see are trees but what you think is wind. When you are driving along a highway and white streamers reel and writhe in snakelike fashion across the bare pavement, or when from the high plough banks bordering the thoroughfare a flowing white cloud completely obscures your passage, what you see is snow but what you think is wind. When you awake some morning after a storm and the first beams of the rising sun shine upon sparkling drifts moulded and shaped in gracefully curving lines, you know that the sculptor has been that almost tangible entity, the wind.

It is little wonder that in primitive societies this sometimes malevolent force was credited with personality. Sir James Frazer in *The Golden Bough*[13] cites examples from many parts of the world of

13 Frazer (1854-1941), Scottish social anthropologist who studied comparative mythology and religion. *The Golden Bough* (first published in 1890) was his defining work.

attempts to fight with actual weapons against the raging tempests. Let me read you one paragraph:

> Often the stormy wind is regarded as an evil being who may be intimidated, driven away or killed. When storms and bad weather have lasted long and food is scarce with the Central Esquimaux, they endeavour to conjure the tempest by making a long whip of seaweed, armed with which they go down to the beach and strike out in the direction of the wind crying "Taba" ("It is enough"). Once when northwesterly winds had kept the ice long on the coast and food was becoming scarce the Esquimaux performed a ceremony to make a calm. A fire was kindled on the shore and the men gathered around it and chanted.
>
> An old man then stepped up to the fire and in a coaxing voice invited the demon of the wind to come under the fire and warm himself. When he was supposed to have arrived, a vessel of water, to which each man present had contributed, was thrown on the flames by the old man, and immediately a flight of arrows sped to the spot where the fire had been. They thought the demon would not stay where he had been so badly treated. To complete the effect, guns were discharged in various directions and the captain of a European vessel was invited to fire on the wind with cannon.
>
> On the 21st of February 1883 a similar ceremony was performed by the Esquimaux of Port Barrow, Alaska with the intention of killing the spirit of the wind. Women drove the demon from their houses with clubs and knives with which they made passes in the air; and the men, gathering around a fire, shot him with their rifles and crushed him under a heavy stone the moment steam rose in a heavy cloud from the smouldering embers on which a tub of water had just been thrown.

Now we know that such an attempt to allay the force of the winter wind is an exercise in futility and that all we can do is to dress warmly and grin and bear it. But we also know that the time is not far distant when the ice will run in the river and the snow will melt away and buds will burst and burgeon as the birds return at spring's bidding. And there will be days when we will hear a rustling from the tree branches no longer bare and watch green waves rolling through the fields and what we will see will be leaves and grass but what we think will be — ahh, the summer wind!

A Past Visit From The Governor General

1979

The recent induction of Canada's new governor general[14] reminded me of accounts given in our local press of occasional visits to New Brunswick of former representatives of the Crown. One such visit to Woodstock took place in the summer of 1873,[15] and although the notice was short, the occasion was made memorable by the cooperation of the whole community. There were guards of honour, parades, hastily assembled but effective decorations, and a suitable address of welcome by Mayor Lewis Peter Fisher, who said:

> May it please Your Excellency, we the mayor, councillors, and inhabitants of the town of Woodstock, beg to assure Your Excellency of the very great pleasure it affords us to have the honour of welcoming to our town and province one so eminently qualified as Your Excellency to represent our most gracious sovereign the Queen.
>
> It is with pride and gratification that we witness Your Excellency, called to the exalted and responsible position of Governor General of this Dominion while yet in its infancy, and while but a dim perception of its immense possibilities is beginning to dawn upon us, making yourself acquainted by personal observation with the local character and wants of our confederacy. We feel assured that the information thus gained, coupled with your administrative ability of the position of which

14 Prime Minister Pierre Trudeau had appointed Ed Schreyer, former NDP premier of Manitoba, to the position of governor general.

15 Lord Dufferin, Governor General of Canada 1872-78, was the first viceroy to travel extensively throughout the country, visiting every province during his tenure.

Your Excellency's past life has given undoubted proof, will cause your period of rule in this Dominion to be marked in our annals as one in which the foundations of our national success and prosperity were laid sure and steadfast.

Having now left the seaboard of our province, having turned your back upon the great commercial marts and penetrated into the interior, thus evincing a desire to become personally acquainted with all our various resources, Your Excellency cannot expect to find such manifestations of cumulative wealth as has greeted you elsewhere. But we believe Your Excellency will perceive, as you travel through the country, evidences of our possessing such agricultural capabilities, and such natural facilities for transport — the true basis of a country's greatness — as cause it to compare favourably with almost any other land, producing as it does, not only the real substantials of life in abundance, but also a hardy, intelligent race of men and women, who, as is proved by their numerous churches and school houses, and by their conduct whenever opportunity offers, show that they fear God, love their country, and honour the Queen and her representative.

To Your Excellency and Lady Dufferin, we extend the most cordial welcome and trust that in health and strength you may both be spared to fill a long life of usefulness. We would also offer our somewhat late congratulations on the auspicious event which added to Your Excellency's family a home-born citizen of our Dominion.[16] May her rich dowry be her mother's graces and virtues, and her father's mind, and may the young life begun under our Dominion skies, in a prosperous

16 Victoria Alexandrina, born May 17, 1873, was the sixth of seven children born to Lord and Lady Dufferin, and the first of two born in Canada.

> and happy future, be a bright link in the golden chain, which shall, like the aroma of sweet incense, twine around pleasant memories of Your Excellencies' sojourn in Canada.
>
> Signed on behalf of the inhabitants,
> L.P. Fisher, Mayor.

The Governor General made an appropriate extemporaneous response in which he remarked upon this first public allusion to the birth of his daughter, and promising that "I shall not fail to remind the young lady whenever she shall be able to comprehend the meaning of my words, that the first welcome she received in Canada proceeded from the inhabitants of Woodstock." The Countess accepted flowers graciously and seemed especially pleased at the reference to the vice-regal baby, an item strangely overlooked in their reception elsewhere in Canada.

On leaving the hall, Their Excellencies in a barouche took up the line of march in a procession formed of the band, the fire companies, the steam engine "Woodstock" and hand engine "Rescue" (both tastefully and strikingly decorated), Col. Baird's Rifle Company, and citizens generally.

There were 140 torches in the procession, which paraded the principal streets where windows of stores and private residences were tastefully illuminated, and escorted Their Excellencies to the hotel — when Lord Dufferin called for Chief Engineer Cluff and expressed personally his entire satisfaction with all the arrangements.

So on that occasion in 1873, Carleton County lived up to its traditional reputation for loyalty and hospitality — not forgetting the human touch.

A Vote For The Chickadee

1981

One day last week I was half listening to a newscast in the background and I thought I heard the announcer say that there was a group lobbying to have an official bird chosen for New Brunswick, just as we have an official flower in the blue violet. The bird suggested was the black-capped chickadee. Nova Scotia has apparently already pre-empted the white-throated sparrow which would have been another likely candidate.

I think the chickadee is an excellent choice. He has been around for a long time, he stays all winter, he's bright and attractive, courageous and friendly. Chickadees often produce two large families in a single season so the species is apt to be with us for many years to come.

As a matter of interest I turned to *The Birds of America* to see what John James Audubon[17] had had to say about the chickadee in the 1840s. I almost didn't find out, as Audubon had him listed as the black-cap titmouse. This reminded me that the chickadee's European relative, the marsh titmouse, was considered to be the little bird of the familiar statement, "A little bird told me," which gave rise to the vindictive nursery rhyme:

> Tell-tale tit!
> Your tongue shall be split
> And all the dogs in town
> Shall have a little bit.

I found that Audubon had devoted six pages to the black-cap titmouse or chickadee, and here are some of the things he said:

---

17 Audubon (1785-1851), French-American ornithologist, naturalist, and artist, known for studying and depicting birds of North America. His four-volume work, *The Birds of America,* was first published in 1827.

Hardy, smart, restless, industrious, and frugal, the Black-cap Titmouse ranges through the forest during the summer, and retiring to its more secluded parts, as if to ensure a greater degree of quiet, it usually breeds there. Numerous eggs produce a numerous progeny, and as soon as the first brood has been reared, the young range hither and thither in a body, searching for food, while their parents, intent on forming another family, remain concealed and almost silent, laying their eggs in the hole deserted by some small Woodpecker, or forming one for themselves.

The Black-cap Titmouse, or Chickadee, as it is generally named in our Eastern States, though exceedingly shy in summer or during the breeding season, becomes quite familiar in winter, although it never ventures to enter the habitations of man; but in the most boisterous weather, it may be seen amidst the snow in the rugged paths of the cheerless woods, where it welcomes the traveller or the woodcutter with a confidence and cheerfulness far surpassing the well-known familiarity of the Robin Redbreast of Europe. Often, on such occasions, should you offer it, no matter how small a portion of your fare, it alights without hesitation, and devours it without manifesting any apprehension. The sound of an axe in the woods is sufficient to bring forth several of these busy creatures, and having discovered the woodman, they seem to find pleasure in his company.

A woodcutter in Maine assured me, that one day he happened to be at work, and had scarcely hung up his basket of provisions, when it was observed by a flock of these birds, which, having gathered into it at once, attacked a piece of cold beef. After picking until they were tired or satisfied, they left the basket and perched directly over his fire, but out of the direction

> of the smoke. There they sat enjoying themselves and ruffling their feathers to allow the warmth more easy access to their skin, until he began his dinner, when they immediately alighted near him, and in the most plaintive tones seemed to solicit a portion.
>
> Often indeed have I watched the busy Chickadees, as they proceeded from tree to tree, and from branch to branch, whether by the road-side or in the interior of the forest. The light rustling sound of their concave wings would intimate their approach as well as their retreat, as gaily one after another they passed onwards from one spot to another, chattering, peeping everywhere, and determined as it were, not to suffer a chink to pass without inspection.
>
> The Chickadee feeds on insects, their larvae, and eggs, as well as on every sort of small fruit, or berries, including grapes, acorns, and the seeds of various pines. I have seen them eat the seeds of the sunflower, the pokeberry, and pears, as well as flesh of all kinds. Indeed it may be truly called omnivorous.

Audubon goes on to describe the chickadee's fur line nest and talks about its various calls, and it's obvious from the tone of his account that he thought highly of the bird.

I have very much enjoyed the winter company of chickadees at wood splitting sessions or on walks up the driveway, and they inspire a sense of pleasant expectation when the time comes that they stop repeating their own name and turn to the plaintive three note strain that sounds for all the world as though they were saying, "Spring's coming."

I'd be very happy to cast a vote for the chickadee as the official bird of New Brunswick.[18]

---

18 The black-capped chickadee was proclaimed as the official bird of New Brunswick in August 1983, following a contest conducted by the provincial Federation of Naturalists.

The First Casualty

1979

Not long ago I was listening to an *As It Happens*[19] radio reconstruction of events, personalities, and the general atmosphere of the year 1943. At that time, the war, which was the dominating feature of the era, had begun its turn onto the long road which would eventually lead to victory for the Allies against the Axis powers. Franklin Delano Roosevelt's dry New England voice spoke of success in Africa, Winston Churchill promised the "Nahzees" difficult days and nights, and we heard again the clipped military phraseology of Dwight D. Eisenhower.

I was immediately reminded of the contemporary newscasts, stories, and articles which formed the background for the general impression we retain concerning the nature of World War II — selected, censored reports which formed the stuff of myths and legends to be handed down from generation to generation. Subsequent critical examination of material released following the end of hostilities has enabled writers and historians to assemble more objective and balanced accounts of the significant occurrences during the years from 1939-1945, but it will be a long time, if ever, before they replace the remembered impressions and attitudes.

In 1917, United States Senator Hiram Johnson was quoted as saying, "The first casualty when war comes is truth." In 1975 a special correspondent for the *Sunday Times* in London, England — Australian-born Philip Knightley[20] — completed a book entitled *The First Casualty*. It's an examination of news coverage by war correspondents of conflicts ranging from the Crimean War to Vietnam. The book examines the problems faced by writers attempting to produce realistic accounts of ongoing events and identifies a spate of false propaganda tales and atrocity stories.

19 CBC Radio's weekday current affairs program airing since 1968.

20 (1929-2016), Australian journalist and author.

Anyone conditioned by national pride or misled by the militarily-expedient releases of wartime days will find much disillusionment in the pages of *The First Casualty*. The disturbing thing about this book, and others of a similar nature, is that it leads to questions regarding the credibility of present day news items from the world's many troubled spots. Do we really know what is going on in the struggle between Tanzania and Uganda? Or the conflict between North and South Yemen? What is the ultimate meaning of the new relationship between the United States of America and the People's Republic of China? What is Russia really thinking about events in Vietnam and Laos and Cambodia, and why should there be such extraordinary concern about the defection of an individual familiar with secret documents of NATO?[21] If the hot lines connecting Washington and Moscow and Peking have been in operation, what messages have they been carrying?

When things happen half a world away there's a tendency for us to ignore them in the face of domestic concerns related to economic problems such as inflation and unemployment and the unpredictable dollar, or what will happen in Quebec, or in the forthcoming federal election. And there are enough personal problems in our day-to-day lives to make us forget that the bloodshed and violence in news items is any more real than sequences in old war movies once the TV set is turned off. But the flashback to 1943 set me thinking about the fear of atomic war that pervaded events of the late '40s and the '50s — with Emergency Measures Organizations, directions for fallout shelters, and all the rest of it.

Though that fear has been pushed well into the background we know that the potential is still there and in magnified form. And I continue to wonder, as I hear and read conflicting reports about this revolution and that rebellion, about punitive attacks and retaliatory strikes with the most modern weapons from factories in great power countries, just what is going on in our world and who is making the decisions. I feel a sense of growing personal frustration at being kept in the dark about such things. Secret diplomacy is a fact of life in a competitive and divided world, but I wish there were a way for us to discover the truth now instead of 30 years from now.

21 An apparent reference to the case of Ursel Lorenzen, a West German who worked at NATO headquarters in Brussels and defected to East Germany in March, 1979.

Danger UXB

1981

This is written after a long succession of gray and cloudy days, but in spite of frosty mornings and occasional flurries of whirling snow, there continue to be unusually early signs that the hounds of spring are indeed on winter's traces. Some of the black birds, crows, and starlings have already come back to our part of the world. The other day smoke rising above a distant field drew my eyes in the direction of grass blazing a month or more before the appointed time for spring burning. And one morning I saw a kite high in the sky, bobbing and weaving in the March wind and tugging against the string held in young hands hidden beyond the houses.

It's the wrong time of year to be thinking about war and its ravages, but last weekend on the public television network I watched a documentary recounting the 1940-41 days and nights of the bombing of London by the German *Luftwaffe*, scenes of terror and destruction that seemed magnified in horror by the intervening years of peace. That same evening I watched an episode in the *Masterpiece Theatre* series, "Danger UXB," a story punctuated by moments of almost unbearable suspense as the units appointed to deal with unexploded bombs went about their perilous task of trying to render them harmless. As I viewed the exploits of Brian Ashe and his men I recalled reading somewhere about an unusual trio who had been involved in this dangerous and necessary occupation and my mind probed its memory section until it came up with the name of the author, Winston Churchill. I looked up the appropriate passage and this is what Britain's wartime prime minister had to say on the subject:

> In the middle of September a new and damaging form of attack was used against us. Large numbers of delayed action bombs were now widely and plentifully cast upon us and became an awkward problem. Long stretches

of railway line, important junctions, approaches to vital factories, air fields and main thoroughfares had scores of time to be blocked off and denied to us in our need. These bombs had to be dug out and exploded or rendered harmless. This was a task of the utmost peril especially at the beginning when the means and methods had all to be learned by a series of decisive experiences....

I had always taken an interest in the delayed action fuse which had first impressed itself on me in 1918 when the Germans had used it on a large scale to deny us the use of the railways by which we planned to advance into Germany. I had urged its use by us both in Norway and in the Kiel Canal [in the Rhine]. There is no doubt that it is a most effective agent in warfare on account of the prolonged uncertainty which it creates. We were now to taste it ourselves. A special organization to deal with it was set up....

Special companies were formed in every city town and district. Volunteers pressed forward for the deadly game. Teams were formed which had good or bad luck. Some survived this phase of our ordeal. Others ran twenty, thirty or even forty courses before they met their fate. The unexploded bomb (U.X.B.) detachments presented themselves wherever I went on my tours. Somehow or other their faces seemed different from those of ordinary men, however brave and faithful. They were gaunt, they were haggard, their faces had a bluish look, with bright gleaming eyes and exceptional compression of the lips; withal a perfect demeanour. In writing about our hard times we are apt to overuse the word "grim." It should have been reserved for the U.X.B disposal squads.

One squad I remember which may be taken as symbolic of many others. It consisted of three people - the Earl of Suffolk, his lady private secretary and his rather aged chauffeur. The called themselves "the Holy Trinity." Their prowess and continued existence got around among all who knew. Thirty-four unexploded bombs did they tackle with urbane and smiling efficiency. But the thirty-fifth claimed its forfeit. Up went the Earl of Suffolk in his Holy Trinity. But we may be sure that, as for Mr Valiant-for-Truth, "all the trumpets sounded for them on the other side."

Very quickly, but at heavy sacrifice of our noblest, the devotion of the U.X.B detachments mastered the peril.[22]

22 Winston Churchill, *The Second World War: Their Finest Hour* (1949). The "Holy Trinity" included Charles Henry George Howard, the 20th Earl of Suffolk, Beryl Morden, his secretary, and Fred Hards, his chauffeur. 'Mr. Valiant-for-Truth' is a character in John Bunyan's *Pilgrim's Progress*, Pt.II, Ch. XIII who describes himself as "a pilgrim ... going to the Celestial City."

Walks On The Crust

1982

One morning not long ago, I was in the kitchen of our old house by the river putting down food for the cats, when all of a sudden there was a power failure. Whenever that happens I like to check with the neighbours to make sure the problem is general and not something affecting just us. The March winds had been howling up on the hill and I was afraid that a tree might have fallen across the wires leading down to the intervale. I called the Speers and discovered that their power was off too. Alma Speer and I talked for a few minutes and in the course of the conversation she said, "With the rain and these mild days and cold nights it shouldn't be too long before there's a crust."

That simple sentence brought back a wealth of memories. While I carried on with the morning chores and waited for the power to come back, I recalled the times in late March and early April of years ago when our son Stephen and the Speer children, Robert John and Jane, would set off for hikes "on the crust." Excited by the prospect of exploring areas of the winter landscape that for months had been inaccessible except on skis or snowshoes, they would start out briskly, our dog or theirs for company, with all the exuberance and vitality of youth and all the interest of those who are knowledgeable about the out of doors.

For there were stories to be read from the vast open pages of the snow-covered fields. Here was a set of tracks where a fox had come trotting out of the woods, and there was the place where he had raised up on his hind legs and dropped his forefeet down hard on the snow's surface trying to break through to tunnels where the field mice scurried back and forth. Elsewhere were tracks of other small animals to be identified. A disturbed patch on the white expanse centred by a red stain and tufts of fur embedded in the icy snow could be interpreted as a success story or a natural tragedy, depending on whether you looked at it from the point of view of a predatory hawk or a white-coated rabbit running a zigzag course across the dangerous open field. At the foot of a tree near the wooded hillside might be found pellets of indigestible bones and rodent fur — evidence that a limb of that tree was a favourite roosting spot for an owl.

The bare branches of young trees by the river bank revealed nest after nest of various shapes and sizes which had been hidden by green leaves when the summer birds had built them. And there would still be birds to see or hear: the rude cawing of returning crows, the cries of ravens soaring upward on the thermal cushions of rising air, the scream of the jay, the "hank" of the nuthatch, the peculiar call of a cock pheasant — a sound to follow in hopes of catching a glimpse of the strutting bird in his coat of many colours. Sometimes you might see a group of goldfinches, clad in their drab winter feathers but distinguishable by the erratic swooping of their distinctive flight pattern, or a flock of redpolls settling down on the seed-bearing tops of tall weeds protruding above the crust, or a flurry of snow buntings wheeling as one and speeding out over the frozen river.

When the youngsters returned from one of these expeditions, eyes sparkling and rosy faces beaming, it was fun to listen as they sat with mugs of hot chocolate while words came tumbling out over one another as they talked about their adventures and discoveries.

Last Tuesday morning shortly after the sun had risen above the summit of Sharp's Mountain, paling the ghost of the half moon setting in the west beyond the village, I went outside and tested the snow cover. It had been a cold night and the wind still had "a bit of a knife in it." When I found that the crust was firm enough to bear my weight, I started off up the flat followed by one of the cats — the middle-aged one we call Scamper, all white except for a black spot on her back and a tortoiseshell head and tail. The gales of this windy winter had pocked and pitted the snow surface so that it appeared like a miniature copy of the lunar landscape.

It gleamed in the sunlight as the long shadows shortened, but there was now sparkle as there is after a new snowfall. A succession of sunshiny days had distorted the visible animal tracks, deepening the trails of mice and squirrels and broadening the pad marks of rabbits to the point where the hind feet impressions almost reached the "big foot" size of the legendary Sasquach. I strode along for nearly a mile and then Scamper let me know that she thought we had gone far enough. I turned and retraced my steps — this time against the wind, which seemed to tighten the skin on my face in spite of the increasing warmth of the climbing sun. On the way I stopped to cut a few willow twigs on which the furred catkins were just beginning to emerge.

In our part of the world we must accept the fact that winter will continue to insist upon ignoring the arrival of the vernal equinox — but there is no point in becoming impatient — and much pleasure may be found in late season walks "on the crust," watching for signs of the coming spring.

Spring

The Calendar

1977

March is a month that usually provides plenty of opportunity for conversation on the subject about which, as Mark Twain observed, "everybody talks." The lion-like roaring of the recent blizzard would have been drowned out by the combined comments of all those who made observations about the discrepancy between the arrival of spring according to the calendar, and the actual behaviour patterns of our North American weather. I was reminded by some of these comments that there was a time when, contrary to Mark Twain's further observation, somebody did try to do something about it — not the weather itself, but about the calendar interpretation of it.

During the French Revolution, the founders of the First Republic adopted, in 1793, a brand new calendar with the year one opening of September 21, 1792, the day the Republic began. The interesting thing about that calendar was the descriptive name chosen for each of the twelve months. They started with the last nine days of September and most of October under the name *Vendémiaire*, the vintage month, and then came *Brumaire*, the misty month, and *Frimaire*, the month of frost. The winter months were: *Nivôse*, the month of snow, *Pluviôse*, the rainy month, and *Ventôse*, the month of wind. Spring brought: *Germinal*, seed time, *Floréal*, blossoms, and *Prairial*, the meadow month. While summer was made up of: *Messidor*, a harvest period, *Thermidor*, a time of heat, and *Fructidor*, the month of fruit. Before starting off again with *Vendémiaire*, there would be five supplementary days, six in the leap year, which would be devoted to National celebrations. This calendar was used in France until it was abolished by Napoleon I on January 1st, 1806.

Nowadays there are many people who seek to escape some of our North American weeks of false spring by actual flight. If we were to alter our present calendar so that all the months were of 30 days or less, we might adopt a supplementary period for this time of year under the name of Florida or Bermuda or the Caribbean. But all of us can't be follow-the-sun commuters and, seriously, there is nothing wrong with this time of year in the Maritimes if only we would stop expecting it to be what it is not.

For every day of lingering winter discomfort there is a day of promise when the warm sun quickly melts the fallen snow. Maple sap is already flowing and children of many a rural family are tapping trees for the sheer fun of seeing gallons of sap become cups of sweet syrup on the kitchen stove. From now on, almost any day might include the arrival of one or another of the early migrants and we'll see and hear again birds that have been long away. Incidentally, those who have been putting out food for the winter birds should not stop now just because their stock of seeds and suet may be running low. Your regulars have come to count on your handouts and might be in trouble if these should stop before Nature adopts a more provident attitude herself. And sometimes the early newcomers can be greatly helped by your continuing generosity.

At this uncertain season of the year there are bound to be some days when, by the time you step out the door, the earlier rising sun will have dispersed the night's frost and there's an indefinable sense of expectancy that permeates your being with every breath of the morning air. If we possess ourselves in patience, the experience of the real spring, when it comes, will be all the more pleasurable for these teasing times between the March and April days of late snow and mist and cold rains which give the lie to the calendar.

A History Of Kites

1980

The other day I was driving up the road to Upper Woodstock and I noticed, caught on a limb in one of the tall maple trees surrounding the Upper Woodstock cemetery, what appeared to be the tattered remains of a kite.

The sight set me thinking about what it had been like as a boy to hold in my hand a twine-wrapped stick, and to feel the pull of a kite swaying high in the blue sky of early springtime, wagging its tail in the late March wind. There would have been the long runs down the open field and perhaps a couple of false starts and diving failures necessitating adjustment of tail or bridle before the collection of sticks and string, paper and paste soared upward and took on a life of its own. I remember the round stick twirling in my two hands as the ball of twine grew smaller and smaller and the kite rose higher and higher — and I experienced a sense of power in my ability to set limits upon its flight for freedom. It was fun too, sometimes, to send messages into the air by fastening a piece of paper to the kite string and watching it run all the way up to the moving, straining object which I held in bondage.

As I drove along the road I wondered how many centuries of coming spring times had been heralded by flying kites. I knew the ancient Greeks had flown them as early as 300 BC. When I got home I decided to do a little research on the subject. I discovered that one tradition has it that kites were invented by the Greek scientist Archytas of Tarentum four centuries before the Christian era. But it is known that the people of Asia have been kite flyers from as far back as there is any record, and probably even before that. In some cases the practice had religious significance, and it was believed that kites flying over a house at night would ward off evil spirits.

From time immemorial there have also been practical uses for kites. Oriental generals were known to have used them as signals, and signal kites are supposed to have been a feature of the Battle of Hastings, in 1066 when William of Normandy conquered King Harold and changed the course of English history. Kites have carried lines across streams, and cables attached to the lines have marked the beginning of bridges. Lines flown to ships wrecked near the shore have made possible the rescuing of stranded passengers, and men marooned on ice floes have owed their salvation to a kite-borne rescue line. Every young physics student is familiar with Benjamin Franklin's notable experiment in 1752, when he hung a key from a kite line during a storm and demonstrated the electrical nature of lightning.

For many years, before being superseded by balloons and airplanes, kites were used to carry weather observation instruments aloft. The record height for this purpose was reached by a train of ten kites at Mount Weather, Virginia on May 5th 1910 when an altitude of 23,835 feet was recorded. During the last century numerous attempts were made to build man-carrying kites for observation purposes and in 1894 Capt. B.S.F. Baden-Powell lifted a man 100 feet with a 36-foot kite. In Baddeck, Nova Scotia, during the early experiments with flight, Alexander Graham Bell and his young associates Baldwin, McCurdy and an American officer, Lt. Selfridge, built a number of kites. In 1907, Selfridge, lying in a recess in the centre of a large 208-pound tetrahedral kite constructed of 3,393 cells, was lifted into the air to a height of 168 feet behind a small steamer which towed the soaring structure over the lakes for a flight that lasted all of seven minutes. Many years ago I talked to some of the women at Baddeck who had sewed together the small tetrahedral cells that went into the making of that kite, and they told me about the tireless work that went into those early attempts to free man himself from the restricting force of gravity.

So, kites have and a long and varied history, and I suspect that even now there are youngsters comparing notes on the merits of the different types of string-held identifiable flying objects. It won't be long before our late winter runs out of gales and blizzards and other ammunition for its rearguard action and no doubt there will again be kites in the sky as a sign of spring in 1980.

Keep Feeding The Birds

1982

One obvious result of this year's old-fashioned weather is that the wild birds owe more than usual to those who have been kind enough to provide food for them during the winter months. Things even out though, and I am sure that the time, trouble, and expense has received full compensation in the pleasure to be found in observing the feeder guests.

At the Clarke house in Woodstock the feeder is placed on an iron pole near the clothesline platform. It's in full view of the kitchen window and I can remember late last fall, after the feeder had been cleaned and filled, being called to the window to witness the coming of the first customers. A half dozen chickadees had flown from the patch of woods behind the house and sat side by side on the clothesline taking turns at the mixture of wild bird seed and sunflower seeds in the feeder. Shortly afterwards a flock of tree sparrows, the kind Audubon[23] called Canadian Buntings, made the first of many daily visits. You can identify them by the little dark stickpin on their breasts, something like the one the song sparrow wears in summer.

Over the long winter, not a day passed without there being something to watch from the vantage point of that kitchen window: quarrelling blue jays scattering as much seed to the ground as they picked up in their beaks; a single white-breasted nuthatch smooth and sleek in his natty costume, hanging in an upside down position from the top of two seed-encrusted suet balls in a mesh bag suspended from the clothesline, and pecking away at the bottom ball — until he was ousted by the downy woodpecker who came to take his place; a lone blast-beruffled starling who arrived during the coldest days of January to eat his fill and then sit huddled in a doorway corner out of the wind, absorbing the meagre warmth of the midwinter sunshine.

23 John James Audubon. See: "A Vote for the Chickadee."

We worried about that starling. He was with us only a few days before he disappeared. We hoped that he had joined other starlings, rash enough to stay all winter, roosting on the edges of the chimney pots to beat the bitter cold.

Conspicuous by their absence this year have been the evening grosbeaks, beautiful though unmannerly creatures, but they are unpredictable in their seasonal movements, and it's often a case of one year you have them, the next year you don't. We've also missed the purple finches of other years, with their sprightly movements and raspberry-stained breasts. But this lack has been supplied by the flock of redpolls that first came in February and has been around ever since. The pigeons discovered us late this year, but now a baker's dozen arrive twice daily, lining up along the steaming shed roof and fluttering down for the chicken scratch I scatter in the yard. They are variously marked, some of them quite interestingly, and the spring sunshine emphasizes the iridescence of the feathers around their necks.

There are some people who may be apt to think that with the arrival of warm sunshine and the dropping of the snow level it is no longer necessary to put out food for the birds. This is decidedly not the case. Our visitors have come to depend on our daily handouts and it will be some time yet before an abundance of natural food can take their place. If your seed bag is getting low, don't expect to make it do — go and buy a new one.

The presence of available food can also be of great assistance to some of the first birds arriving from the south. You may look out your window any time now to see a mixed flock of blackbirds responding gratefully to your early season largesse, or the graceful figure of a mourning dove among the strutting pigeons! I can remember a winter of deep snow when an early surge of warmth brought back innumerable birds who were in deep trouble when the thaw was succeeded by a prolonged flow of arctic air into the region. I watched robins out on the snow crust, trying to find surviving sustenance from the tiny wormlike creatures crawling along in the snow, and there was a high mortality rate among warblers who had been hoodwinked into premature migration.

Anyone who has held in his hand an injured bird has felt surprise that a creature so light in weight and so small in substance under the feathered coat can express such vitality in movement, such fierceness in action, such challenge or sheer joy in the quantity or quality of song. In the natural scheme of things, we are aware of the debt we owe to the avian representatives of the life force. Whatever we can do for them is never too much.

Walks With A Three-Legged Cat

1977

The other day I had a really good look at a plump partridge walking among dwindling snowdrifts, a red squirrel digging out butternuts, and a white-breasted nuthatch running straight down the trunk of a venerable spruce tree. I might have missed them all if it hadn't been for our three-legged cat.

About four years ago, this particular member of our feline family roamed a bit too far afield and was hit by a car on the highway. One of our neighbours reported having seen her by the side of the road and my wife Dees went up and brought her home. After an unsuccessful attempt to save her badly smashed leg, the vet decided that an amputation was necessary and he performed it. When she had convalesced sufficiently to walk outside, we agreed that her trips abroad should be supervised, so that she wouldn't go up to the highway again. She's getting along in years and if four good legs couldn't save her from an accident, she wouldn't have much chance at all with only three. In many cases, I have been her companion.

She would often start off at a great rate, scuttling along over the causeway between the ponds, and then she'd stop to roll in the summer dust and catch her breath for a while. It was during these rest pauses that I learned to look for what there was to see. I'd sit quietly by the side of the road and light my pipe and, in a few minutes, the apparently-deserted surroundings would suddenly teem with life. I'd watch small rodents darting across the road, or spot a chipmunk's bright eye peering from the top of a mossy rock. A pair of courting cedar waxwings might come sidling along the branch of a maple tree, touching their bills in tentative caresses. And the silence that had greeted our arrival at that particular place would be broken by a resumption of sounds: birdsong of many kinds, or the rat-tat drumming of a woodpecker's bill.

Never before had I been quite so conscious of what Pope spoke of as "the green myriads in the peopled grass."[24] Looking down between my feet, I'd see all sorts of insects resuming their briefly interrupted functions. Once I watched an ant carrying an egg moving frantically down the hill — now pulling, now pushing — over pebbles and around rocks, and I wondered what tragedy had led to his apparent flight and whether he knew where he was going with his salvaged load.

Sometimes, part way along her usual route, my charge would slip over the side of the driveway into the long grass to prove that she could still catch a field mouse. Near the place where I waited for her was a stagnant pool left by the lowering pond. What seemed at first a barren patch of murky liquid became a setting for dramatic action as living creatures moved in spurts over the surface or swam in the shallow depths, hunting and being hunted in their small predatory universe.

Since the day I first started those walks I have often, on other occasions, made it a point to take a good look at people and things that had previously occupied only a peripheral place in my vision or my attention. There were streets in town that I seemed to be seeing for the first time as I took in the architectural details of the old houses: and, on a summer morning, as Main St. came to life, I found that there were things to be learned from the casual words of greeting exchanged with friends and acquaintances, or from the expressions on the morning faces of familiar strangers. In the woods and fields, I've often benefited from the knowledge that the investment of a few minutes' silent waiting yields many more of interesting observations.

I still enjoy going for interrupted walks with our three-legged cat and, over the years, I have come to agree with the conclusions of the "supertramp" poet, and to realize more exactly what he meant when he composed the verses that began:

> What is this life if, full of care,
> We have no time to stand and stare?[25]

---

24 Alexander Pope (1688-1744), English poet. *An Essay on Man: Epistle I*

25 William Henry Davies (1887-1940), Welsh poet, lived a vagrant lifestyle, wandering and pursuing adventure, such as hopping a train to the Klondike Gold Rush, only to lose a foot. In 1908, he published *The Autobiography of a Super-Tramp*. Quoted here is a verse from his poem, *Leisure*.

Ice Cakes And Common Sense

1979

Part of the way of life for those who live beside a great river is the annual springtime concern about how the river will behave at break-up time and during the run-off freshet period. It's when those with long memories enliven story telling sessions with tales of rampaging ice floes and high-water experiences in days long gone. In the past, in my part of the province, these exchanges were generally free from elements of bitterness or recrimination, any inconveniences caused by occasional freshet flooding being chalked up as "acts of God."

But it's not like that today. Now, the people of the river, as they keep one eye on the March or April weather and the other on the St. John's frozen surface, wonder what effect the Mactaquac headpond will have on each spring season's time of crisis. Three major floods in half a dozen years have taught many of them to ignore coincidence disclaimers from the Power Commissioner and conversational responsibility has been shifted from the deity to the increasingly omnipotent entity which harnessed and attempts to control the St. John River. I've heard them talking this week.

"In the old days," they say,

> when the ice broke up and started to run it had somewhere to go, and we used to go down and stand on the old bridge and watch those great flat cakes come sailing by, some as long as aircraft carriers with big bow waves and a trailing wake; and they'd smash against those bridge piers with a sound like thunder and then on they'd go and more would come along behind them. Oh we'd watch for hours. But now the ice hits that headpond and shoves and pushes and smashes and piles up in a great slow-moving jumbled mass and it's just common sense that it's more apt to

> jam and that when it jams the water's going to rise behind it, and there we are like now with the water running back up the crick and the bridge closed and Water St. flooded, and it isn't even full freshet time yet. And if it's like this now what would it be like if they try to raise that thing another three feet?

That's the voice of people who remember the plans and the promises of the early 1960s, people who will be skeptical of similar reassuring and mystifying explanations, couched in terms of graphs and charts and flow figures and kilowatt hours against which their only weapon is common sense. For these people with their particular concerns, and for many others for other reasons, any reduction in public accountability for a government agency on the grounds that such accountability would hinder the carrying out of planned projects is a matter of concern — particularly because some of those projects, like the raising of the headpond, are still extremely controversial issues.

The availability of energy is of extreme importance, but experience has shown that assessment of the cost of its production should not be left entirely in the hands of those who are responsible for producing it. Over the years this fact has been recognized in public participation on an advisory basis, but politically and otherwise there is still too much power in the hands of the power producers. There is no question as to their dedication to their task, but that very dedication can blind them to important considerations and sometimes to the dictates of what the old-timers sum up as "common sense."

April Bridges To Spring

1978

The month we know as April was probably given its name by Etruscans in the ancient days, even before they ruled the little village men called Rome. In any language it's an unsettling time of year, inspiring moods that range from dark depression to ecstatic heights. Over the centuries, unnumbered poets have tried with mixed success to trap the essence of the season in immortal rhyme, and the range of phrases underlines the versatility of April's image in the minds of men. She has been named the "cruelest month," and "peevish," with days of "uncertain glory" not to be trusted, capable of swift anger but with a wonder that's worth it all — blooming, beaming, beneficent, and much more besides.

When I look back over the ages, the poet who most comes to mind this time of year is Geoffrey Chaucer, and I can almost see him by a sunny window some six centuries ago plying his pen to tell of an English April's sweet showers and fragrant breezes, bringing forth the flowers of spring, while "smale foweles" or little birds make constant melody, and man himself shares nature's restless urge to get going along the road of some self-imposed pilgrimage.[26]

Here in our part of the St. John River Valley, April has lived up to her reputation as a tease, with heavy frosts succeeding warmer hours — but change is in the air. We have watched the brown leaves emerge along the lower slopes of hillsides, and higher up the trees stand in ever widening cleared circles among the banks of shrinking snow.

A couple of weeks ago the black birds came in flocks to add their chatter to the sound of crows — cowbirds and grackles and red-winged blackbirds. One day last week I saw a great blue heron standing with slumped shoulders on a cake of ice beside a small patch of open water in

26 Chaucer (c.1343-1400), English poet, wrote *The Canterbury Tales*. Its prologue begins by remarking on April's springtime activity.

a St. John River tributary creek, looking as though he were wondering why he had come so soon. Then, just last weekend, the robins arrived in force, hopping about on half-cleared lawns and emerging garden plots. Someone said they had seen a morning dove — someone else a killdeer, and then the other morning I heard the welcome sound of song sparrows singing cheerily by the bank of the still frozen river.

A couple of nights ago just after supper, I caught the scent of burning grasses in the April air, a sign that soon we'll be watching the lines of flame leaping and dancing and marching over fields and hillsides in the annual grass-burning ritual that is itself a sign of spring in this part of the country. Boys swinging branches or wet bags will help to keep the fires under control, and there will be shouting and laughter, black boots and soot stained faces, the stimulant of danger should the wind begin to blow, a sense of conflict with the flying flames, and a final satisfaction in the knowledge that the black terrain will soon be green with new growth for the summer days ahead.

The other day in the hardware store in town, the man in front of me at the counter saw me looking at the fish hooks which were part of his order. "I know it's early," he said with a grin, "but a fellow should be ready when the time is right — and it won't be long now." The sound of running water is everywhere these days, gurgling and rippling in drains and ditches, as ice and snow respond to the alchemy of April sunshine.

Why is it, I wonder, that some people feel in springtime the same unexplainable sadness that others experience during autumn days? Perhaps they share the emotions of the 20-year-old young man in Housman's poem who felt that the 50 springs remaining to him were hardly enough to fully appreciate the wonder of the blossoming cherry trees.[27] Perhaps it is that the mighty natural forces soon to be released in root and bird and bursting seed exert an influence upon mankind beyond our understanding, and some feel sad because the true significance of what is happening seems just beyond their reach. But most of us accept the eccentricities of April with cheerful and forgiving hearts, looking forward as we do to the pleasure of her promises.

27 A.E. Housman (1859-1936) English poet, wrote *Loveliest of Trees.*

Afternoon Tea

1980

A few days ago I was present in my mother-in-law's kitchen just after she had come down from her afternoon nap. As is customary about that time, the kettle was boiling and tea was steeping in the brown pot. Mrs. Clarke poured us both "a nice cup of tea" and while the hot liquid helped to dispel the memory of the cold March-like April winds outside, we started speculating about the origins of such a pleasant afternoon custom and wondering, among other things, whether the historic Boston Tea Party of 1773 had anything to do with the American preference for coffee. When something we're curious about comes up for discussion, sooner or later there is recourse to a reliable source of information, and in this instance I discovered the following quotation:

> The colonists' resentment of the role played by tea in their bickering with the mother country created an unfavourable image of the beverage, an image from which it never fully recovered. By mid-20th century, Englishmen were consuming about five times as many pounds of tea as coffee, while Americans were consuming about 25 times as many pounds of coffee as tea.

While I had the appropriate volume of the encyclopaedia in my hands, I read some other interesting information about "the cup that cheers." There is a Japanese myth which credits the origin of tea in China to the plight of a Buddhist saint, who is supposed to have remained seated before a wall in meditation for nine years. During one of his meditations the saint fell asleep and upon awakening he was so upset that he cut off his eyelids to make sure that it wouldn't happen again. He cast the severed eyelids to the ground where they miraculously took root and grew as the tea plant, whose leaves when infused in hot water, produced a beverage that was capable of banishing sleep.

The Chinese themselves date the introduction of tea as a beverage to the reign of the mythical emperor Shen Nung about 2,700 BC. It was in the 17th century AD that the stay and comfort of the Englishman's "castle" arrived in the tight little island. England was the greatest coffee-drinking country in the world when tea was first publicly sold at Garway's Coffee House in London in 1657, advertised as "That excellent and by all physitians approved China drink."

The English East India Company played a major role in the introduction of China and India teas into England and colonial America, and in popularizing the beverage. But the custom of taking afternoon tea first came to the New World not from England but from Holland. It was introduced in New Amsterdam, now New York City, and with it came the teaboards, teapots, silver spoons, strainers, and other tea table items that were the pride of Dutch housewives. Milk was not used at first but New Amsterdam hostesses offered sugar and sometimes saffron and peach leaves as flavouring agents for tea.

In England, the custom of serving afternoon tea and cakes was originated by Anna, Duchess of Bedford, about 1840.[28] Till then most Britons consumed a huge breakfast and didn't eat again until eight o'clock at night. But the example of the Duchess resulted in widespread acceptance of the new meal with tea and cakes at five o'clock. Today the people of Great Britain and Ireland are generally considered the world's greatest tea drinkers, consuming about ten pounds per person annually. In Australia and New Zealand, annual per capita consumption varies from seven to eight pounds. Canada is the foremost tea-drinking country of the Western Hemisphere. We account for about three pounds per person per year as compared with the half a pound that satisfies our coffee loving neighbours below the border, and a lot of that half pound goes into the making of summertime iced tea. Being great compromisers, many Canadians start the day off with coffee for breakfast and switch to tea for later meals.

---

28 Anna Russell, 7th Duchess of Bedford (1783-1857), was a life-long friend of Queen Victoria.

One of my favourite memories associated with the traditional brew is the refreshment it brings after a long day's paddle when the kettle is boiled on a beach over an open fire. Now that's an occasion that merits the use of the word "comfort." The formal afternoon teas of other days have become social history now, but I'm glad that in most homes it's still considered appropriate when mid-afternoon rolls around to boil the kettle, scald the pot, see what's left in the cookie tin, and spend a few pleasant minutes over a "nice cup of tea."

George Brown On Confederation

1980

In these days when we are hearing so much about the troubles that beset our nation, and amid gloomy predictions of its imminent dissolution,[29] it is interesting to look back at the situation which prevailed just before Confederation. The other day I was reading some of the 1865 Confederation Debates held in what was then the Province of Canada. The Honourable George Brown[30] began his major speech with these words:

> Mr. Speaker, it is with no ordinary gratification I rise to address the house on this occasion. I cannot help feeling that the struggle of half a life-time for constitutional reform — the agitations in the country, and the fierce contests in this chamber — the strife and the discord and the abuse of many years — are all compensated by the great scheme of reform which is now in your hands. Here is a people composed of two distinct races, speaking different languages, with religious and social and municipal and educational institutions totally different; with sectional hostilities of such a character as to render government for many years well-nigh impossible; with a constitution so unjust

---

29 Following the victory of the Parti Québécois in the Quebec election of 1976, the government of that province pursued a policy of separation from Canada. In 1980, a hotly-contested provincial referendum was held in which a majority voted against separation, although the debate over the topic would continue for many years.

30 George Brown (1818-1880) was a Father of Confederation, founder of the *Globe* newspaper (later to become *The Globe and Mail*), and a fierce political rival of John A. Macdonald. Brown, Macdonald, and George-Étienne Cartier would join forces to lead a coalition government in establishing Confederation throughout British North America.

in the view of one section as to justify any resort to enforce a remedy.

And yet, sir, here we sit patiently and temperately discussing how these great evils and hostilities may justly and amicably be swept away forever. We are endeavouring to adjust harmoniously greater difficulties than have plunged other countries into all the horrors of civil war. We are striving to do peacefully and satisfactorily what Holland and Belgium, after years of strife, were unable to accomplish. We are seeking by calm discussion to settle questions that Austria and Hungary, that Denmark and Germany, that Russia and Poland, could only crush by the iron heel of armed force. We are seeking to do without foreign intervention that which deluged in blood the sunny plains of Italy. We are striving to settle forever issues hardly less momentous than those that have rent the neighbouring republic and are now exposing it to all the horrors of civil war.

Have we not, then, Mr. Speaker, great cause of thankfulness that we have found a better way for the solution of our troubles than that which has entailed on other countries such deplorable results? And should not every one of us endeavour to rise to the magnitude of the occasion, and earnestly seek to deal with this question to the end in the same candid and conciliatory spirit in which, so far, it has been discussed?

After putting forward at some length arguments in favour of the proposed Confederation, Mr. Brown concluded:

Sir, the future destiny of these great provinces may be affected by the decision we are about to give to an extent which at this moment we may be unable to estimate — but assuredly the welfare for many years of four millions of people hangs on our decision.

> Shall we then rise equal to the occasion? Shall we approach this discussion without partisanship, and free from every personal feeling but the earnest resolution to discharge conscientiously the duty which an overruling Providence has placed upon us?
>
> Sir, it may be that some among us will live to see the day when, as the result of this measure, a great and powerful people may have grown up in these lands — and when one united government, under the British flag, shall extend from shore to shore....

There was of course opposition to some of the provisions of the proposed scheme then, as there are critics of today's greatly amended constitution — but in coming debates and decisions regarding the future, it is to be hoped that men will remember the corporate accomplishments, as well as the problems, of the past 113 years. May they also be as visionary in their context as was D'Arcy McGee[31] when he said:

> I see in the not remote distance, one great nationality, bound, like the shield of Achilles, by the blue rim of ocean. I see it quartered into many communities — each disposing of its internal affairs — but all bound together by free institutions, free intercourse, and free commerce; I see within the round of that shield, the peaks of the Western mountains and the crests of the Eastern waves — the winding Assiniboine, the five-fold lakes, the St. Lawrence, the Ottawa, the Saguenay, the St. John, and the Basin of Minas — by all these flowing waters, in all the valleys they fertilize, in all the cities they visit in their courses, I see a generation of industrious, contented, moral men, free in name and in fact — ever capable of maintaining, in peace and in war, a constitution worthy of such a country.

31 Thomas D'Arcy McGee (1825-1868). This quotation is from a speech delivered in 1860, debating constitutional changes. See also: "A Canadian Assassination."

A Canadian Assassination

1981

Canadian listeners and viewers shared with citizens of the United States the feelings of horror and dismay that came with the news, reporting the attempted assassination of President Reagan.[32] Over and over again we watched the videotape showing the President departing from the hotel and the events which followed in a space of seconds — shots wounding the chief executive and leaving three men lying on the sidewalk. It was the sight of James Brady face down with a bullet in his brain that reminded me of an assassination that is a part of our Canadian history.

It took place shortly after two o'clock in the morning of April 7, 1868 on Sparks St. in Ottawa, and it brought to an abrupt end — a week before his 43rd birthday — the life of a Father of Confederation whose celebrated eloquence had been most influential in converting public opinion to the idea of federal union. The victim was Thomas D'Arcy McGee.

Born in Ireland on April 13th, 1825, he emigrated to America at the age of 17 where he made a precarious living as a journalist and lecturer. Before he was 20 he was persuaded to recross the Atlantic and take a position in London as a correspondent for Dublin papers championing the cause of Irish freedom. Here in libraries and in the press gallery of the House of Commons he increased his general knowledge and his capacity for political oratory. When the Young Ireland movement staged an abortive revolt in 1848, McGee, though he had not carried arms, fled again to America disguised as a priest. He continued his journalistic work in New York, Boston,

32 On March 30, 1981, John Hinckley Jr. shot US President Ronald Reagan as he was leaving a Washington, DC hotel following a speaking engagement, wounding him seriously. He required immediate surgery and made a full recovery. Three others were wounded in the shooting including Reagan's press secretary, James Brady, who suffered permanent brain damage.

and Buffalo but finally, somewhat disillusioned by a growing American antipathy to Irish expatriates, he moved to Montreal in 1857. He began his political career as a member for Montreal in 1858. Sitting first as an independent he eventually joined forces with Macdonald's government serving as Minister of Agriculture from 1864 until Confederation.

But his fame as a Canadian lies in his contribution to the union cause. Acknowledged as one of the most gifted and persuasive orators ever to sit in Parliament, his public and private word pictures of national possibilities had a profound effect in the Canada of his day and in the Maritimes on his frequent visits here. Along with his vision of the future, he warned of present danger from the current belief, supported by many Americans, "in the fulfillment of our manifest destiny to overspread the continent." He warned, too, of the danger of invasion by the Fenian Brotherhood[33] and urged that preparations be made to repel it. The invasion of 1866 was a failure, but McGee's words of warning were the cause of his death.

In this case the assassin was crazed not by psychiatric disorders but by alcohol, as he said while in prison: "Whisky is the devil. If it were not for whisky, I would not have shot McGee. I was as drunk as the devil when I did it." Pat Whelan, a Fenian supporter, made many a drunken boast in a Montreal drinking establishment that he would shoot McGee if he had a chance and finally some of his pals called his bluff and provided him with the chance — a weapon, money and lots of whisky. After failing to carry out his boast in Montreal, Whelan followed McGee to Ottawa.

On the fatal night, Whelan listened in the visitors gallery as McGee spoke eloquently attempting to allay Nova Scotian opposition to the young Confederation, promising to conquer the province with kindness and calling on Canadians to work together amicably toward a radiant future. When McGee stepped out into the frosty, moonlit April night with a couple of his colleagues, Whelan followed. McGee

33 An organization of Irish nationalists formed in the United States in the 1860s under John O'Mahony. Fenian invasions in various parts of Canada had as their aim the seizure of territory for use in negotiations with the United Kingdom to secure the independence of Ireland.

said goodnight his corner, made his way alone to Mrs. Trotter's lodging house, and was just putting his key in the lock when Whelan moved up behind him and shot him in the head. The alarm was raised and a doctor called but McGee was pronounced dead at the scene. Sir John A. Macdonald helped to carry his friend's body into the house. The next day's *Ottawa Times* account included the following paragraph:

> Our heart is too full for utterance on such a horrible event, with the sound of the fatal shot almost ringing in our ears; it will send a thrill of horrors through the heart of every Christian man, not only in the wide Dominion of Canada, but wherever the English language is spoken, and in every country of the civilized world. The martyr McGee will take his place in history among the brightest and most noble victims ever cruelly sacrificed by ruffian hand because of devotion to their country.[34]

34 *Ottawa Times*, Tuesday April 7, 1868

Cold Turkey & Other Curiosities

1982

One afternoon at teatime, the conversation around the kitchen table at the Clarke house turned to the presently popular subject of "giving up smoking." The various approaches toward that admirable aim were being discussed and evaluated when somebody said, "The only successful way is to quit cold turkey." The chief result of the conversation from my point of view was that my curiosity was aroused about the origin of the phrase "cold turkey." I lit my pipe and went to see if I could find out about it. It wasn't difficult to find "cold turkey" defined as "abrupt complete cessation without medication of the use of drugs by a drug addict," but nowhere could I find a derivation. Why "cold turkey?"

When I mentioned my problem to Mrs. Clarke a few days later she told me that during a recent visit to Montreal she had been asked by someone why bread and butter pickles were called "bread and butter pickles." She didn't know for sure but conjectured that perhaps it was because they tasted good with just bread and butter. I tried to look that one up too and once again I could find a definition but no derivation. Could it be that those sliced cucumber pickles were considered suitable for ordinary everyday use and as common on the table as bread and butter? Or is there some other explanation? One might even make a case for considering them as company fare if you interpret the phrase "bread and butter" in the sense of "hospitality" as it's used for "bread and butter letters."[35]

In any case, my bump of curiosity is now itching in two places and I realize how many words and phrases there are which we use every day, but don't know from whence they came. In the course of

35 Much as a host would put bread and butter on the dinner table, the rules of etiquette required guests to write a letter of gratitude for the hospitality received. Because of the regularity of this exercise, these notes became known as bread and butter letters.

my fruitless search for cold turkey and bread and butter pickles, I did learn about some other things. My wife sometimes wears a pair of blue jeans made of denim. I know now that the word "jeans" comes from "jene," a kind of cloth originally acquiring its English name from a French appellation (*Genes*) for the Italian city of Genoa where the cloth was made. The original English form of "denim" was "de Nim" and it was first applied to a twill serge cloth manufactured at *de Nîmes*, the capital of the department of *Gard* in southern France.

Several centuries ago *de Nîmes* was already noted for its extensive textile industry and *serge de Nimes* was known throughout the western commercial world. In 1695, the *Merchants' Magazine*, published in London, listed serge denims that cost six pounds each and five years later the *London Gazette* referred to a pair of flowered serge denim breeches! "Denim" is now applied to the twilled cotton cloth we associate with overalls and jeans.

Another discovery I made was how Jimson weed got its name. Jimson in this connection is a corruption of "Jamestown" and Jamestown weed received its name from the fact that it was found growing in abundance around Jamestown in colonial Virginia. Early in the spring this weed sprang up in the rich ground under the very shadow of the buildings that the settlers had erected on the tiny island in the James River. The weed is also known as thorn apple, devil's trumpet, and stinkweed. It belongs to the nightshade family, is highly poisonous, and its leaves yield the official drug stramonium, used in certain medicines, tonics, and compounds for heart ailments.

The narcotic properties of this plant were known to the Algonquin Indians as well as the Aztecs of Mexico, both of whom used it as a ceremonial intoxicant. In his *History and Present State of Virginia* published in 1705, Robert Beverley[36] tells an interesting story of the effect that eating Jamestown weed had on some of the British soldiers sent over to suppress Bacon's Rebellion in 1676. I quote:

---

36 Robert Beverly Jr. (c.1667-1722). This work is regarded as the first published history of a British colony by a native of North America. The rebellion was an early example of revolutionary sentiment, pitting young Nathaniel Bacon against Gov. Sir William Berkeley, his cousin, through marriage.

> Jamestown weed being an early plant was gathered very young for a boiled salad by some of the soldiers sent thither and some of them ate plentifully of it, the effect of which was very pleasant comedy, for they turned natural fools upon it for several days. One would blow up a feather in the air, another would dart straws at it with much fury and another, stark naked, was sitting up in a corner, like a monkey, grinning and making mows at them; another would fondly kiss and paw his companions and snear in their faces with a countenance more antick than any in a Dutch Droll.
>
> In this frantick condition they were confined lest they should in their folly destroy themselves, though it was observed that all their actions were full of innocence and good nature. Indeed, they were not very cleanly for they would have wallowed in their own excrement if they had not been prevented. A thousand such simple tricks they played and, after eleven days, returned themselves again, not remembering anything that had passed.

After such a trip you would think that the hapless Redcoats would be very willing to quit taking Jimson weed "cold turkey."

Old Joe Bite

1977

In a recent issue of *The Bugle*, published in Woodstock, there appeared as part of the "75 Years Ago" column a brief item concerning one Joe Bite. Old Joe was an Indian who lived at Upper Woodstock and the item disclosed with regret that in the first week of May, 1902, he had been stricken down with paralysis in his legs and was now laid up in his hut. At that time he was well over 100 years of age and, to quote the article, "enjoyed the reputation of being the oldest man in the Dominion."

The location of Joe Bite's hut was at the mouth of Lane's Creek where, at the turn of the century, a number of Indians had their humble dwellings on land adjoining the southern boundary of our place. The location was a traditional Maliseet camping ground. My late father-in-law, Dr. G.F. Clarke, discovered a number of prehistoric stone artifacts there, and once when he and his friend Tappan Adney were exploring the site, they came upon a circle of fire stones. Mr. Adney somewhat arbitrarily concluded that they were part of an ancient Indian sweat bath. When and how the transition was made I do not know, but I do know this same circle of stones is presently on display in Prince Edward Island.

But to get back to Joe Bite. He was not of the Maliseet tribe but had come to this country as a young man, married, and remained here even after his wife's death. His real last name was something that sounded like Alain, but it was rarely used after he became an old man. He existed then mostly on charity and always carried with him an Indian basket laden with the practical results of the imploring question, "Have you got a bite for Joe?" Hence the name Joe Bite. Over the years he became known to everyone in the area as something of a character.

My friend Dr. Peter Paul was in for a cup of tea the other day and we got to talking about Joe Bite. Peter was a boy of three when the old Indian died, but he had since heard many stories about the old man. As a matter of fact, in a portfolio of historic snapshots Peter had with him was one of a family group with Joe Bite sitting in the centre. This was the family which had taken Joe to live with them at Lower Woodstock, after illness had at last disabled him. Peter said he'd been told by old Fred McCloskey that Joe was a member of the Black Snake tribe. He took this information with a grain of salt at the time — never having heard of that tribe — but a few years ago a visiting priest who had been studying church history told Peter that he had found a record of a Mission situated near the conjunction of the boundaries of New Hampshire, Vermont, and Quebec. The Indians there had been known as the Black Snakes. Whatever his origin, Joe Bite, partly perhaps because of his longevity, made a lasting impression on the minds of his contemporaries.

In the old days, most communities had their quota of "characters," sometimes objects of scorn and derision, sometimes of pity and compassion, sometimes even of a non-conformist, Huckleberry Finn kind of envy. They were much discussed during their lifetimes and long remembered after their passing. If you were to ask me why the death of one of these apparent failures should affect the members of a community, I would have to say it was because the community would never be quite the same again with old so-and-so gone. Somehow you imagined him to be impervious to time and change and you were somehow surprised that he was not.

Dr. Clarke once told me that after old Joe Bite was taken to Lower Woodstock, he disappeared one day. The family who harboured him looked everywhere for him without success. Finally, someone journeyed to Upper Woodstock and there, sure enough, was Joe Bite in his hut by the Creek.

His friends spoke to him gently saying he'd better come home.

"No," the old man said, "Home right here."

"But Joe, if you stay here you'll die."

"Well," said Joe, "home good place to die from."

When he did die shortly afterwards, I suppose you could say that the public reaction to the news of his passing was a homely example of John Donne's observation on mankind and mortality which concludes: "And therefore never send to know for whom the bell tolls; It tolls for thee."[37]

37 John Donne (1572-1631), English poet. From *Devotions Upon Emergent Occasions*, Meditation XVII.

Defence Of Fort 96

1978

After the American Revolutionary War, when Loyalists were coming to what is now New Brunswick, it was decided that the lands on the St. John River above what is now Fredericton should be granted to soldiers of Provincial Regiments. This area had previously been kept free from settlement as a lumbering preserve — the great pine trees on the slopes above the river providing ideal masts and spars for the King's Navy. The Provincial Regiments had been raised by loyal Americans to fight side by side with the British Redcoats against their rebellious countrymen and bore such names as the King's American Dragoons, Loyal American Legion, Queen's Rangers, and so on.

In the area where I live now, grants were made in the parish of Northampton on the other side of the river and in the parish of Woodstock on this side to members of de Lancey's Brigade, raised by a New York businessman, Oliver de Lancey. The other day I was reading about some of the exploits of this active unit during the war and I came across one action that had, in reality, all the elements usually employed in fictional re-creations of military adventures. Let me give you an outline.

In the month of May, 1781, Lt.-Col. Cruger of de Lancey's Brigade was commissioned to proceed to Fort 96 near Camden, South Carolina and prepare the fort for defence. He was supplied with a garrison of 550 men: 150 of de Lancey's Brigade, 200 New Jersey Volunteers, and 200 loyal militia under Col. King. He had but few cannons, was short of ammunition, and the defences of the post were in a very unfinished state when the American Gen. Greene appeared on the scene with an attack force of 4,000 men. Four thousand against 550.

The action began on the night of the 21st of May, 1781, when besiegers broke ground and threw up two earthworks within 70 paces of the fort. But while they were engaged in strengthening those works, the following night a party of the garrison rushed forth to the attack. Every man of the pioneer party was put to the bayonet, the works were demolished, and even the entrenching tools were carried off. Such sorties became a regular feature of the positive defence in the days ahead.

When Gen. Greene peremptorily called upon the garrison to surrender in the face of such great odds, Col. Cruger answered that Fort 96 was committed to his charge and that it was his duty, as well as his inclination, to defend it to the last extremity. When the besiegers fired from their muskets arrows with combustible material flaming at the tip in an effort to set the barracks afire, Cruger calmly ordered his men to de-roof the buildings in order to save them.

Continual cannon fire gradually took its toll and near the middle of June, when the outworks of the fort had been almost completely demolished, the defenders retreated behind the main stockade after successfully repelling an attack by a party attempting to set fire to the outworks. The main problem now was that the garrison was cut off from its water supply and attempts to dig a new well in the fort were unsuccessful. Undaunted, a number of blacks in the garrison volunteered to strip naked and crawl to a water source near the American lines. At critical moments they would lie still, indistinguishable from a number of logs scattered over the area. In this way a scanty but sufficient supply of water was maintained. During the trying weeks, Col. Cruger was everywhere, encouraging his men by word and example to die in the last ditch rather than surrender.

Finally, on the 17th of June, the defenders saw a lone horseman riding at full gallop through the American lines to approach the fort in a hail of bullets. His welcome message was that Lord Rawdon was in full march with a force to raise the siege. The cheer that greeted these words alerted Gen. Greene to the need for immediate action and at dawn the next day a major attack stormed toward the fort. As their advance group hit the trench under the wall, a group of New Jersey Volunteers lead by Capt. Campbell jumped down among them at one end of the trench and a group of de Lancey's led by Capt.

French dropped from the stockade at the other end. Shouting their war cries, they charged along the trench, their bayonets clearing all before them. Gen. Greene beheld with astonishment his design foiled by the desperate valour of a mere handful of men and he could not persuade his force to make another attempt. As the rebels left the scene, the sound of bugles in the distance announced the arrival of the relief force.

Such was the calibre of some of the men who came to find new homes after the war along the St. John River.[38]

38 This essay is based on an account of the battle written by W.O. Raymond (see note 9, p. 27) in the Woodstock *Dispatch* between 1894-96

Fiddleheads

1979

On the first Sunday in the month of May some lines by Shakespeare come to memory:

> The nightingale, if she should sing by day
> When every goose is cackling, would be thought
> No better a musician than the wren.[39]

I remembered these lines as I wondered whether the succulent spring greens we call fiddleheads would be as ardently anticipated by New Brunswickers if the season for picking them were to be shifted to the month of July, or even to August. I had just parked the half ton at the foot of our driveway, where the base of the wooded hillside on our place meets the ponds that once were fields, when I noticed that the warm sunshine after days of rain had already begun its annual alchemy: the transmutation of seemingly dead black plants into a source of emerging tightly curled green fronds.

I took a large paper bag from behind the truck seat and started picking with the usual feeling of excitement and pleasure, even though I ran into resistance from the omnipresent hawthorns. I sometimes feel that these armoured shrubs harbour a personal antipathy toward me. I get along very well with most growing things, and I have tried to remember whether I was ever guilty of mistreating a hawthorn tree, because whenever I approach one now I'm inevitably repeatedly scratched by the long black needles in spite of care and caution. But oh! how symbolic was the green sight of the new fiddlehead growth, and the distinctive taste of the munched raw stem and the peculiar springtime fragrance of the folded ferns.

Part way up the hillside there's a rocky ledge some 15 feet high and at its base there's a broad area of lace-like green growth from which

39 Portia, in *The Merchant of Venice,* V, i.

protrude slight stems each bearing a row of Dutchman's breeches. As I straightened my back and looked toward them I noticed that the fiddleheads were not the only newcomers to the hillside. Already there were a number of purple trilliums in full flower — a touch of rich colour above the floor of brown leaves and needles to compensate for the blossom's shortcomings in its contribution to the sense of smell. As if on cue, there came a rolling trill from over the flooded field to remind me that the name wake-robin is also used for these magic-number flowers. And near at hand, here and there on the warm southern slope, were golden dogtooth violets or adder's tongues or trout lilies, depending on your favourite name for them, with mottled leaves of green and brown. Now I believe all this is an important part of fiddlehead picking.

My friend Dr. Peter Paul tells me that the curved motif that is a distinctive feature of Maliseet decorative art is in fact a representation of the fiddlehead. For the ancient people, he told me, the fiddlehead was medicine as well as food — a highly respected spring tonic. And I suspect that it was even more than that, coming as it did so soon after the tribesmen were reunited. Separated of necessity during the winter months, each small party had made its way from cold season hunting preserves to the shore of the freshet-swollen river where they had cached their canoes in the fall. Then came the swift descent to the summer quarters on the long intervale at Meductic and scenes of joyful reunion. The tales of adventure and tragedy and triumph of the season past would take days in the telling, and there'd be stories left to follow the feast of fresh fish and fiddleheads which made it clear that the new and happy season had at last been well begun.

When my bag was full, I plucked one each of the new spring flowers to take home with me as a sample to show my womenfolk. The fiddleheads, cleaned and cooked, were a welcome addition to our planned Sunday dinner with Aunty Ruby and Mrs. Clarke.

As I tasted them, I came to the conclusion that they would indeed be delicious if picked in July or even in August; but, at the same time, my mind completed the Shakespeare quotation in Portia's words:

> How many things by season, seasoned are
> To their right praise and true perfection.

Summer

Thunder & Lightning

1978

Time and time again during the last hot weather week of the month of May, the sky over the St. John River valley shared expanses of clear blue with towering thunderheads. Now the sun gilded the soaring tips of cumulus cloud masses and again the sky would darken as their blue-black curtain obscured the blazing rays. Occasionally, the warm breeze would stop blowing and over the land a sudden hush would fall, broken only by peals of distant thunder. Here and there, up and down the valley were brief but heavy showers, hard driving drops bouncing from pavement or the surfaces of swiftly formed puddles, showers that soon ended, affording little relief from the hazy heat.

The awesome atmosphere of these often repeated threatening periods set me thinking and reading about thunder and lightning and man's reaction to them from the early days. It's little wonder that such displays of raw power were considered to be of divine origin, weapons of retribution wielded by Zeus or Jupiter, or the teutonic Thor among many others. The Hebrew prophets saw in lightning the divine will of Jahweh and the psalmist spoke of the voice of his thunder quelling the waters that first covered the earth. The early Christians believed that blasphemy and related sins would bring forth primitive and punitive bolts of God's revengeful lightning.

Dramatic poets down the ages aroused pity and terror in scene after scene of violent storm: Shakespeare's Cassius baring his bosom to the thunderstorm on the tempestuous night before the death of Caesar; King Lear, "a poor, infirm, weak and despised old man" raving against the raging elements —

> You sulphurous and thought-executing fires,
> Vaunt-couriers to oak-cleaving thunderbolts,
> Singe my white head! And thou, all-shaking thunder,
> Smite flat the thick rotundity o' the world![40]

40 *King Lear*, III, ii.

"Oak-cleaving thunderbolts"— the phrase was used in conformity with the widely accepted belief that certain trees such as oak, ash, poplar, and fir attract lightning. On the other hand, the hawthorn, laurel, aspen, beech, and elder were thought to repel it. The folklore of many nations extends immunity from lightning bolts to pregnant women, to those who are sound asleep, and to infant children. Those awake in storms could seek magical protection from sacred objects such as the Bible, candles, bells, and salt. It was once believed that the safest place to be in a thunderstorm was in a feather bed.

My modern authority gives the following advice, and I quote:

> It is best to be indoors, to avoid contact with the telephone, electrical equipment, and water systems, and to sit away from the fireplace. If one is caught outdoors, sheltering in a forest is fairly safe, but isolated trees should be shunned. At the sea or lake, swimmers should leave the water and yachtsmen stay below deck. Proximity to long metallic conductors, such as wire fences, ski lifts, and railway lines is dangerous because of voltage transfer and induced surges. However, during a thunderstorm it is exceptionally safe inside motor cars and railway trains.

End of quotation.

The long, scientific explanations of what causes thunder and lightning are interesting and reassuring, but when the sudden hush falls over the darkened land and a violent storm is about to begin, most of us can understand the emotional origins of the ancient myths.

Chautauqua

1977

In one of the letters I've received in connection with this program was the following question: "Do you remember what it was like when the Chautauqua used to come to Woodstock in the old days?" The answer to that would have to be, "No," but I certainly do remember when the Chautauqua came to Yarmouth, Nova Scotia, when I was a boy.

Its arrival was greeted with general excitement, not quite the same kind of excitement as when the circus came to town, but something close to it. We young folk would watch the big tent going up in a field that was within sight and earshot of our backyard and we'd look forward to participating in the activities of its week-long stay.

I can remember sitting inside the tent listening to the lady who conducted the children's story hour. There was a special atmosphere in the place compounded of sunlight diffused by the canvas roof and walls, the gentle stirrings and flappings in the big enclosure caused by the summer breeze, and the sound of the story lady's trained voice capturing our imaginations and involving our emotions. She made everything seem so real. You could feel us all straining in sympathy with the little engine slowly moving up a steep gradient puffing out its self-encouraging, "I think I can, I think I can, I think I can," and our group sense of relief and triumph as it rattled down the other side saying, "I knew I could, I knew I could, I knew I could!"

I can remember a kite-making contest in which my sister won a prize for one of the prettiest kites — it was decorated with paper flowers — and I recall my disappointment when I didn't get my clown-face kite in on time because I couldn't find out where to take it as an entry. And there were rehearsals in the field with the physical director for the drills and gymnastic displays we boys would take part in on the stage in front of an audience on children's day. I was small in stature but pretty good as a gymnast and was chosen to be top man on the collapsible pyramids. I can still feel the pre-performance internal butterfly flights inspired by the first sight of a large audience from the wings, and the glow of pride and accomplishment heightened by the stirring sound of applause after the act was over.

I remember a "growing-up" feeling of satisfaction in being taken to some of the evening sessions of musical performances; and the impact of the first play I had ever seen on a real stage with live actors. It was *Smilin' Through*[41] and, at the last, in the death scene, when the young and handsome spirit of the hero rose from a seat at the table to join the blue-eyed wraith of the long-dead heroine at the garden gate, I was moved to tears. And I was scared, too, when I realized that the old man at the table was now dead also. It was several nights before I could get to sleep without thinking about it.

The Chautauqua got its name from an adult education institution founded in 1874 at Fair Point on Chautauqua Lake in upstate New York. Originally a training school for Sunday school teachers and church workers, it gradually broadened to include general education and popular entertainments. The use of tents at the original site suggested the possibility of the travelling Chautauquas, and in the peak year of their existence in the United States, 1924, some 10,000 North American communities were visited and total attendance topped the 40 million mark. Circuit Chautauquas declined after the mid-twenties. There was competition from motion pictures and radio, automobiles made transportation to larger centres easier, and a more sophisticated public followed other avenues of instruction and entertainment. In 1932, fewer than 300 communities were visited by Chautauquas and the Depression finally sounded their death knell. But in their day they

---

41 *Smilin' Through,* written by Jane Cowl and Jane Murfin, premiered on Broadway, December 30, 1919, where it ran for 175 performances. The play was the basis for three movies of the same name, including one nominated for an Academy Award for Best Picture in 1932.

made a real contribution to the summer lives of millions of people in thousands of North American communities.[42]

I would like to thank the lady of the letter for reviving for me the young boy sitting on the back steps in the long, green twilight of a summer evening, listening to the sound of a marimba band or the keening lament of a Highland bagpipe, drifting over the fields from the big tent, and thinking about things that might never have been a part of his youthful experience if the Chautauqua hadn't come to town.

42 Although the "Circuit Chautauqaus" no longer exist, the Chautauqau Institution continues today in its original location in New York with a focus on the arts, religion, education, and recreation. Numerous unaffiliated organizations, including one in Nova Scotia, remain faithful to the principles of the movement and are part of the current-day "Chautauqua Trail."

Monster Clouds & Frigid Weather

1982

Last January, Japanese scientists reported the discovery of a mysterious cloud circling the earth about ten miles above its surface. It stretched from the equator to about 50 degrees north, along a line passing through Germany, Poland, and several of the United States including Washington, Idaho, and Montana. American scientists of the National Aeronautics and Space Administration (NASA) began an investigation of the cloud's nature, testing samples of material collected by high-flying U-2 reconnaissance aircraft. Their findings ruled out the possibilities of it being the result of a nuclear blast or meteorite explosion, and they concluded that volcanic action must have been the source of the mystery cloud.

A NASA representative explained it this way: "A typical pattern with a volcano is that it ejects ash, rock, and lots of sulphurous gases. Within the first week all the ash and rock falls out, leaving behind the sulphurous residue that hangs around for months and eventually turns to sulphuric acid." And, he added, "The cloud could cause slight reductions in temperatures on earth for a time due to the high reflectivity of the sulphuric acid droplets." It is believed that the volcanic eruption which produced the cloud must have taken place last winter in Asia, Africa, or somewhere in the ocean. Over a month ago now another volcanic eruption that we do know about took place in Mexico,[43] causing widespread devastation on earth and producing what meteorologists are now calling "a monster cloud."

On a national TV news item the other night a NASA reconnaissance pilot reported that he had never experienced anything like it. Not to be able to see the sun at 68,000 feet was something new for him.

---

43 *El Chichón*, in southern Mexico, was active in the spring and summer of 1982, and the site of the largest volcanic disaster in modern Mexican history.

The cloud is apparently spreading steadily northward and American meteorologists are stating that in addition to some spectacular sunsets and unusual twilights, there could be appreciable temperature effects and the possibility of unseasonably early frosts. A Canadian weather expert interviewed in Toronto was skeptical about such a result, contending that measurable differences in temperature would only amount to two or three degrees.

My interest in all this stems from what I have heard and read about the year 1816, which used to be referred to as "eighteen hundred and froze to death" or "the year without a summer." In 1816, in the northern American states and in southern Canada, there was frost and snow in every month of the year and similar unseasonable weather prevailed in the British Isles, France, Spain, and other parts of Europe.

I have listened to handed-down stories in various parts of the Maritime provinces about how many cattle had to be slaughtered because there was no hay, and the survivors, and humans too, had to be content with turnips and other root crops because grain did not ripen. On the 3rd of October 1816, the Rev. Frederick Dibblee, Anglican rector of the Parish of Woodstock, in his report to the Society for the Propagation of the Gospel,[44] included this paragraph, and I quote:

> It is with regret that I advise the Society of the unhappy situation of this country. Till within three years, no new country within my observation ever made greater progress in clearing the wilderness and acquiring property by honest labour and industry alone, without having any capital. But the third year past the crops were greatly injured by frost. Last year a cold summer and frost deprived us of at least half our crops. But this year, the hand of Providence has fell on us for our sins.

44 Rev. Dibblee (1753-1826), Anglican minister who resided in Woodstock, NB from 1792 until his death. From 1790 onward he worked on behalf of the Society, which was chartered by William III in 1701 as a missionary organization of the Church of England to function in the American colonies (still active today as the United Society Partners in the Gospel). Dibblee's own diary for October 1816 contains a phrase "Never was there such a Summer and Fall."

> Never so cold a spring. On the 9th day of June it snowed almost the whole day. Only one month during the summer free from frost. And before the grain could get ripe the frost fell so hard as to ruin it entirely.
>
> It is supposed by good judges that there is not three months' bread in the country, taking in every particular, barley only of our grain excepted. And what adds to our bad fortune, the crops are so short in the United States that the price of bread will be beyond the reach of the poor, for it is supposed that it will be great indeed. The price of flour is £3/10 per barrel, and nothing but the cash. Unless our government does not provide in time for the necessities of the country, the poor, the widows and the fatherless must suffer and, I fear, to death, for those that are lacking are not able to help them, especially in this distant part of the province. There is a large French settlement 90 miles above us on the road to Canada who have lost every kind of sustenance.

One widespread theory was that the year with no summer was somehow caused by the eruption of the volcano Tomboro, on Sumbawa, an island near Java. In 1815 Tomboro exploded, killing 50,000 people, producing a flow of six cubic miles of lava, and causing a cloud that filled the upper atmosphere over large parts of the earth for nearly a year.

Naturally, what I am wondering now is who is right about the possible effects of the present "monster cloud," the American meteorologists or the Toronto optimist. Only time will tell.

Keeping A Family Journal

1979

Every once in a while when my wife and I are trying to remember the exact date of some event that happened in our area a number of years ago, Dees will say, "I know, I'll call the Speers," and she'll phone our next door neighbours who will consult their family journal and the information will be there. Whenever this happens, we realize all over again how valuable such a journal can be in chronicling the history of a family and a community, and we indulge in self-recriminations about our own shortcomings in this direction. We've made sporadic beginnings, but we have yet to form the habit of making regular entries in a day-book of passing events.

I was considering the value of passing along to listeners, especially young members of new families, the suggestion that they would derive much future pleasure and profit by embarking upon such a venture, when I remembered vaguely that Montaigne[45] had given some advice on the subject about 400 years ago. It has been some time since I'd read any of the famous essays, but I took down Volume I from the bookshelf, got my pipe going ,and turned back the front cover.

For the next few hours I was lost. I had forgotten how much wisdom and common sense were compiled in those pages, how many references to interesting events of ancient history. The author, when he arrived at his 38th year, resolved to dedicate to study and contemplation the remaining term of his life, and as he read and reflected he acquired the habit of setting down his thoughts just as they occurred to him. Those thoughts became a book, the first draft of which appeared in 1580, a new departure in the field of literature. The unusual, for that time, nature of the book is indicated by an introductory note by the author to the reader. Here's what Montaigne wrote:

45 Michel de Montaigne (1533-92), French essayist and humanist.

> Reader, thou hast here an honest book; it doth at the outset forewarn thee that, in contriving the same, I have proposed to myself no other than a domestic and private end: I have had no consideration at all either to thy service or to my glory. My powers are not capable of any such design. I have dedicated it to the particular commodity of my kinsfolk and friends, so that, having lost me (which they must do shortly), they may therein recover some traits of my conditions and humours, and by that means preserve more whole, and more life-like, the knowledge they had of me. Had my intention been to seek the world's favour, I should surely have adorned myself with borrowed beauties: I desire therein to be viewed as I appear in mine own genuine, simple, and ordinary manner, without study and artifice: for it is myself I paint. My defects are therein to be read to the life, and my imperfections and my natural form, so far as public reverence hath permitted me. Thus, reader, myself am the matter of my book: there's no reason thou shouldst employ thy leisure about so frivolous and vain a subject. Therefore farewell. From Montaigne, the 12th June 1580.[46]

But thousands of readers over the centuries have ignored that facetious farewell. When I finally put down Volume I and resisted the temptation to reach for Volume II, I was impressed by the modernity of so many of the opinions expressed despite the antiquity of the examples used to illustrate them — the opinion about education for example.

Oh yes, I found the passage about the value of keeping a family journal and I highly recommend it to your attention. It reads as follows:

> My father in his domestic economy had this rule (which I know how to commend, but by no means to imitate),

46 *Essays of Montaigne*, "The Author to the Reader," Charles Cotton (trans), W.C. Hazlitt (ed), 1877

namely, that besides the day-book or memorial of household affairs, where the small accounts, payments, and disbursements, which do not require a secretary's hand, were entered, and which a steward always had in custody, he ordered him whom he employed to write for him, to keep a journal, and in it to set down all the remarkable occurrences, and daily memorials of the history of his house: very pleasant to look over, when time begins to wear things out of memory, and very useful sometimes to put us out of doubt when such a thing was begun, when ended; what visitors came, and when they went; our travels, absences, marriages, and deaths; the reception of good or ill news; the change of principal servants, and the like. An ancient custom, which I think it would not be amiss for every one to revive in his own house; and I find I did very foolishly in neglecting it.[47]

47 *Essays*, Ch. XXXIV, "Of One Defect in Our Government."

Personal Names

1980

The other day my wife, my mother-in-law, and I were seated at the table at the end of a meal and we were trying to recall the first name of a character in a television series of a few years ago. This concentration on names set me thinking about them as I haven't done for a long time. I know that my own name, Kenneth Churchill Homer, is made up of a Celtic word that means "leader," chosen because I had an uncle Kenneth; a place name, which was the surname of my paternal grandmother whose ancestors must have lived near a church on a hill; and an occupational name. "Homers" were specialized smiths who made holmes or helmets.

I looked up some information about personal names and discovered that there's a theory which contends that the first words were names based upon cries by which primitive people identified themselves to others. It is generally agreed that personal names have been used since a very early period in human development. There is fascinating material about the use of names at various times and in various parts of the world.

The Anglo-Saxons, as well as some of the other barbarian tribes who were responsible for the downfall of Rome, had a practice of taking two ordinary, unrelated words and putting them together to form a personal name, for example the words for fame and spear — Hrothgar, ancestor of Roger. These, at first, were the only names, as surnames or family names came later. The chief effect of the Norman Conquest of 1066 was to introduce to England the use of a few favourite names, originally Scandinavian but modified by Latin and French usage and by transference into English. This was the source of William, Robert, Richard, and Henry or Harry.

The church protested against the use of the old heathen names towards the end of the 12th century, and from this period dates the popularity in England of such names as John, James, Michael, Mary, Anne, Elizabeth, Catherine, Agnes, and Margaret. The ways in which surnames came to be developed are a story in themselves, and it was during this same period in the middle ages that hereditary family names began to be used, first with the nobility and then generally.

Geographically, the use of family names began in London and other developed districts in the country and then moved outward. The process was scarcely complete by 1500 even for England, and in remote areas of Wales, Ireland, and Scotland the use of family names was not universal even in the 18th century. Many people nowadays are interested in knowing whether their first name has a meaning and, if so, what it is. Although we are warned that it's not wise to trust the accuracy of most name lists with ascribed meanings, I found an old dictionary published in 1912 which contains such a list.

I'll read a few of the names:

Abner – a Hebrew name meaning father of light
Abraham – Hebrew for father of a multitude
Adolf – Old High German for noble wolf
Alfred – Old High German for good counsellor
Albert – Old High German for all bright
Algernon – French for whiskered
Alvin – Old High German for winning all
Ambrose – from the Greek for immortal or divine
Andrew – Greek, meaning strong, manly, courageous
Archibald – an old German name, meaning extremely bold
Arthur – Celtic high or noble
Asa – Hebrew healer or physician
Arnold – Old High German for strong as an eagle
Aubrey – Ruler of spirits

On the distaff side there is:

Abigail – my father's joy
Ada – same as Edith, meaning happiness

Agnes – Greek for chaste or pure
Alice – a princess

And so on.

If you are interested in the meaning of your name, try the reference shelf at your local library. If you like, some day I may read some more of these should we get back to names again.

Wild Strawberries

1980

This week started out for me as strawberry week. I enjoy picking them and I was keeping my ears open for announcements that one or another of the local cultivated strawberry fields was ready for U-pick custom, when my wife, Dees, said, "Ken, Lillian Flewelling tells me that there are lots of wild strawberries this year. She and her son are going out again this afternoon. Would you like to go too?" I agreed that it sounded like a good idea. After lunch I went to pick up Lillian and Chris and we drove across the bridge to the east or other side of the St. John River and a few miles into the back country.

It was a cool afternoon with an occasionally brisk northwest wind and somewhat threatening clouds playing tag with the sun. When we stopped at the side of a country road we found that indeed there were lots of berries and that the ground was dry enough to kneel on without discomfort. I hadn't seriously picked wild strawberries for half a century, except for a casual handful on a country walk, and I experienced a certain amount of frustration in the contrast between this endeavour and the ease with which I could fill a quart box in the cultivated fields. As I worked along among the daisies and devil's paintbrushes, I thought about the pleasure that the bright berry had brought to people in so many parts of the world, since it grows in temperate and cool climates just about everywhere.

And I could imagine the delight of 17th century pioneer immigrants to New England when after weeks at sea they found a hillside dotted with the familiar red clusters. To this day, that spot in what is now the city of Portsmouth is still known as Strawbery Banke, the site of an important historical restoration.[48] And the find represented more than

---

48 Strawberry Banke was settled in 1630 and named after wild strawberries growing along the bank of the Piscataqua River, which forms part of the boundary between Maine and New Hampshire.

just a taste treat since any nutritionist will tell you that strawberries have more vitamin C than an equal quantity of lemon; that a handful of fresh picked strawberries supplies an adult man's entire day's need of vitamin C, and more vitamin A than the same weight of raisins.

I had made a couple of trips to the truck to empty the contents of my picking box into a larger container when I was accosted by Lillian who had noticed the results of my efforts. "Ken," she said, seriously, "I see that you are not stemming all your berries as you pick them." And I said, "Well, I found that I was squashing them when I tried to do that and besides, they were bouncing back out of my fingers, and between that and the fact that every once in a while a long blade of grass reaches out and snatches a berry away from me I must have provided a pint for Mother Nature for every two I got for myself." "Well," she said, "that's all part of it isn't it? If I'd known you hadn't picked wild strawberries for a long time I'd have spoken to you before. You have to get rid of the stem and hull as you pick them or they'll be all mushy if you try to do it later. Now, you put your box down and use both hands, hold the stem in one and take off the berry with the other."

After that informative lecture things went better. A kind gentleman stopped his car a few minutes later to tell us that we'd find berries in a field just down the road where there was little long grass and he even escorted us to the place. For the rest of the afternoon we worked away, the breeze, for the most part, keeping off the swarms of midges and blackflies. The sun appeared and disappeared and my fingers and the knees of my corduroy jeans grew redder and redder. Whenever I rose to stretch my legs, there was the grand view of the surrounding countryside and the mountains of Maine visible in the misty distance beyond the hidden river.

My reward that evening was the dish of wild strawberries and cream we had for dessert, and there are half a dozen bottles of wild strawberry freezer jam labelled for use on special winter occasions. The next morning I heard that Roland Dickinson was opening a field to the public, and it wasn't long before I was on my knees again harvesting the large fruited strawberries that had their origin in Europe in the 18th century. Europeans had cultivated the woodland strawberry for years without improvement in size and succulence until species from the New World were crossed with those of the old.

In the warm sunshine of the early morning I reached my quota of eight quarts in jig time, and that evening I sat before a dish of Dees's special shortcake biscuits generously spread with crushed berries and topped with whipped cream. On the shelf was a double batch of cooked strawberry jam along with a number of cartons for the freezer, and I concluded somewhat smugly that our strawberry season for 1980 had made an auspicious start.

Of Yard Sales & Attics

1979

Wherever you go in this day and age it seems, from the signs, that someone, somewhere, will be holding a yard sale. As far as I can gather, these began as individual efforts by people who wanted to clear out their premises and perhaps make a little money on the side, but have now also been taken up on a large scale by clubs, societies, church groups, and other institutions as fundraisers. The difference between the yard sale and the traditional rummage sale seems to be in the nature of the merchandise. The rummage sale offered chiefly clothing and small articles easily transported to the site, whereas the yard sale also handles furniture, appliances, tools — just about anything imaginable.

One reason for the institutional shift to the yard sale approach is that rummage sales, or thrift sales as they later came to be called, are no longer as profitable as they once were. The segment of the population which made up the chief customers and principal beneficiaries of such sales contains many welfare recipients who no longer have the desire or feel the necessity to purchase second-hand clothing. I suspect that lately, especially in smaller communities, there are many instances where pillars of society have ended up buying one another's contributions to the thrift sale in order to ensure its financial success.

One accomplishment claimed for the yard sale is that it has provided a solution to a grave problem arising from the fact that styles of architecture have changed drastically while human nature has not. Our sanitary landfills, or dumps, or whatever you want to call them, are used more than ever these days, but many people are still reluctant to discard items which they think might have a certain amount of value, or that they might find useful someday, even though there is no use for them at the moment. In today's households, where do you put such things? The garage holds only so much if you want to leave room for the car, and many basements have been converted into playrooms, and there is no attic.

In the old days it was different. Such items were relegated to roomy house attics or shed attics and remained there, sometimes for generations. Often, as they lay there in the quiet darkness, a metamorphosis took place in which the valueless discarded items of one era gradually assumed importance as being representative of that era for inhabitants of a later one.

And who can overestimate the educational value of a well-stocked house attic? Many of you will remember what it was like when, as children, you played in the attic on rainy days: dipping into chests and boxes; dressing up in the clothing of your great grandparents; turning the wheels of wool winders; handling gingerly the weapons of ancient wars; reading about battles long ago in the dusty pages of old books and magazines; and spelling out long contemporary newspaper accounts of events now covered, if at all, by one line in a history book.

Home attics have also been immeasurable help to biographers and social historians. The other day I had occasion to be in the shed attic at the house of my late father-in-law, Dr. G.F. Clarke, and all around me were objects representative of his many interests: birch bark canoes and baskets containing flint chippings, scrapers, and fragments of Maliseet artifacts; a shelf of old history books; literary magazines of the 1920s; a fishing creel; strips of veneer and antiques publications; and other memorabilia reflecting various aspects of the New Brunswick author's multifaceted career.

Today, even existing attics are being invaded as a result of the social pressure of the institutional yard sale, and older objects are joining the modern-day cast-offs on the rapid round from hand-to-hand until they take the inevitable journey to the dump. As time goes on, more and more support will have to be found for existing and future museums. It appears that soon their presently limited facilities will be almost entirely responsible for preserving a tangible record of what is past and passing for the benefit of generations yet to come.

In Praise Of Apples

1980

One afternoon recently, when it was sometime after lunch but not quite time for afternoon tea, my eye fell upon a basket of fruit which contained, among other things, a number of apples. At once my mouth began to water. I picked up one of the apples and the feel of it, firm and round in my hand, plus the fragrance that met my nostrils, released a spate of apple-oriented memories.

I was a boy again, rough bark scratching inside knees and thighs as I shinnied up a gnarled tree at Tusket,[49] gathering green apples in a summer season and chewing them without suffering the traditional colicky penalty. I was in the cool cellar of my boyhood home in midwinter, charged with removing bad apples from barrels to prevent the depredations promised by the old proverb. I could see the huge, hard, cooking variety that my mother used in applesauce and apple crisp and turnovers and apple pies. The smaller, softer, luscious eating apples, and the bronze, grainy russets that lasted very well and so were saved till the end of the season.

Then I was on a ladder stretching up and out for the largest reddest apple on the bough almost out of reach, and I could almost feel the autumn sunshine between my shoulder blades and the hard round of the rung under my instep. I remembered Halloween apples swinging on strings defying efforts to bite them without the help of hands, or apples floating in a tub of water to be won only at the expense of a self-imposed ducking. Most of these were youthful memories which made me wonder whether what author John Burroughs had to say about apples were true. This is what he wrote on the subject:

> The boy is indeed the true apple-eater, and is not to be questioned how he came by the fruit with which his pockets are filled. It belongs to him, and he may

49 A small community near Yarmouth, NS.

> steal it if it cannot be had in any other way. His own juicy flesh craves the juicy flesh of the apple. Sap draws sap. His fruit-eating has little reference to the state of his appetite. Whether he be full of meat or empty of meat he wants the apple just the same. Before meal or after meal it never comes amiss. The farm boy munches apples all day. He has nests of them in the hay mow, mellowing, to which he makes frequent visits.
>
> The apple is indeed the fruit of youth. As we grow old we crave apples less. It is an ominous sign, when you are ashamed to be seen eating them on the street; when you can carry them in your pocket and your hand not constantly find its way to them; when your neighbour has apples and you have none, and you make no nocturnal visits to his orchard; when your lunch-bucket is without them and you can pass a winter's night by the fireside with no thought of the fruit at your elbow, then be assured you are no longer a boy, either in heart or in years.[50]

In spite of Mr. Burroughs, and though the years are against me, I still derive much pleasure from the taste of an apple, and I also believe that for much of humanity this commonest of orchard fruits often represents more than merely something to eat. Think of the golden apples of ancient legend, or of the mixture of moonlight and apples in de la Mare's poem, *Silver*:

> Softly, silently now the moon
> Walks the night in her silver shoon
> This way and that she peers and sees
> Silver fruit upon silver trees.[51]

---

50 John Burroughs (1837-1921), American naturalist and nature essayist. From *The Apple-Eater*.

51 Walter de la Mare (1873-1956), British poet, short-story writer, and novelist.

And I'm sure that John Drinkwater[52] had more than food in mind when garret-stored fruit inspired the verses of *Moonlit Apples*:

At the top of the house the apples are laid in rows,
And the skylight lets the moonlight in, and those
Apples are deep-sea apples of green. There goes
A cloud on the moon in the autumn night.

A mouse in the wainscot scratches, and scratches, and then
There is no sound at the top of the house of men
Or mice; and the cloud is blown, and the moon again
Dapples the apples with deep-sea light.

They are lying in rows there, under the gloomy beams;
On the sagging floor; they gather the silver streams
Out of the moon, those moonlit apples of dreams,
And quiet is the steep stair under.

In the corridors under there is nothing but sleep.
And stiller than ever on orchard boughs they keep
Tryst with the moon, and deep is the silence, deep
On moon-washed apples of wonder.

52 John Drinkwater (1882-1937), British poet and dramatist.

Rhubarb

1977

When you are driving down a deserted country road, you sometimes come across evidence to prove that people once lived along it. Here and there will be a clump of lilacs, and perhaps tiger lilies or some other escapees from old flower gardens gone wild. If you stop to look for foundations and find them, you might discover, not far away, the site of the kitchen garden marked only by a still surviving green row of hardy rhubarb plants. Rhubarb is a very satisfying perennial to have in a vegetable garden. It rarely gets winter killed, it has few serious enemies, and its useful yield covers such a long period of time.

One day when I was pulling some red and green stalks from our row and lopping off the broad leaves, I began to wonder where rhubarb had come from in the first place. After I had washed and cut my harvest and placed it in a saucepan on the stove with a cup of sugar sprinkled over the top, I got out a reference book and a dictionary to see what they had to say about rhubarb. Actually, they didn't say too much, but I found out that the name comes from the old Romans and part of it is formed from the Latin word for "barbarian," which then simply meant "foreigner." I was told that rhubarb grew originally in Asiatic Russia and China and that there were several kinds, some used for the preparation of medicinal drugs and some as edibles. As I took a taste of the now bubbling contents of my saucepan on the stove, I could appreciate how the ancient Chinese must have enjoyed rhubarb, remembering the oriental propensity for sweet and sour flavours.

Speaking of flavours, I remember once some twenty years ago, shortly after we had finally moved from the city to our place in the country, that my wife called me to come and taste "something delicious." "I've found a new green," she said, "Here, try it." I accepted the proffered fork and tried the new green, and it was, indeed, delicious. "Have some more," she said, "there's lots."

But when she told me that her experimental offering was composed of rhubarb leaves, I had a nagging suspicion that, somewhere, I had read a warning against eating them. While I went to get my book on vegetable gardening, Dees called our friend, the late Mrs. A.B. Connell, who knew about such things. The answer was the same in both cases: on no account should one eat the leaves of rhubarb. Their heavy content of oxalic acid renders them dangerously unfit for human consumption. Since then, we've had a family joke about how Dees once tried to do me in with poisoned greens.

One of the meanings in the dictionary dealt with the term "rhubarb" as being used to describe a mob fight or a riot. No derivation was given but I have a theory about that one. In 19th century America, an unsophisticated rural resident was often referred to as "Reuben," which became a kind of generic name for such people and was often shortened to "Rube." In the days of the travelling circuses it was common practice for the circus barkers to short change or otherwise bilk the rubes of country crowds whenever they could. Once in a while this led to real trouble when the victims discovered they had been tricked, and fisticuffs would follow. The rallying cry of the circus hands in those days was a shouted "Hey Rube!" Whenever it rose above the mechanical music of the calliope or the hum of the crowd, the circus men came running from all directions, tent pegs in hand, to quell the disturbance. This is only a theory mind you, but I suspect that the ensuing "rhubarb" owed its name more to the common term for a so-called country bumpkin than to the succulent plant in the corner of his garden.

One good thing about rhubarb is that it's ready to harvest so early in the year, a real boon for those whose jam cupboard is getting bare. Some time ago, when I went into my mother-in-law's kitchen, she was just waxing the tops of seven or eight bottles of new jam. I asked her if it was a lot of trouble to make. "Oh no," she said, "I just pulled a couple of pounds of rhubarb stalks, washed them and sliced them up fine. Then I put three cups of rhubarb in a pot and five cups of sugar, and a medium sized can of crushed pineapple, and brought the whole thing to a boil, which didn't take very long. Then I let it boil three minutes, took it off and added a half bottle of pectin, stirred it, skimmed it, bottled it, and there you are." It was good, too. And if you're short of pickles, rhubarb can also be used with onions and vinegar and spices to make a tasty summer relish that will tide you over until harvest time.

Finally, to add some small shred of philosophy to this somewhat rambling dissertation, let me pass on to you a saying I had from an old Maritimer many years ago. "Some people," he said, "is jest like rhubarb, kinda sour-seeming at first. But if you make a point to sweeten 'em up a little and handle 'em right, they'll turn out to be pretty nice after all."

A Visit To The U-Pick

1976

This summer, apparently, more and more "U-PICK" signs have been appearing near farms and cultivated berry patches, and more and more people have been taking advantage of them. Many growers have found this to be a satisfactory answer to the problem of securing seasonal labour, and the amateur harvesters appreciate the chance to save considerably on the cost of filling their preserve cupboards with jams and jellies and other good things.

There's another dimension, too, that can't be evaluated in dollars and cents. Already, the signs for the picking of corn are up along the highroads. I haven't harvested any corn yet, but I do remember the first time that my wife and our son and I went out to pick our own strawberries about 12 years ago, when it was something new.

We started out very early in the morning, crossed the bridge over the St. John River at Woodstock, and travelled a few miles upriver on the other side. When we reached the field, there were a few local housewives already at work down at the lower end, early as it was. There were dewdrops on the plant leaves, and the straw between the rows was still damp as we began to fill our boxes, but the sun was high enough to warm our backs and a light breeze kept the flies away. Every once in a while we'd straighten up for a brief rest or to empty a full box into the canning kettle, and every time we did there was something to see.

An osprey flew over the river with one eye out for prey but, at the same time, very much aware of the bald eagle soaring high above him as though waiting to steal his catch, if he were lucky. Song birds crossed and re-crossed the field and, though the full choirs of springtime had been broken up by the demands of housekeeping, there was enough music to draw our attention as we tried to identify its makers. Along the borders of the berry patch, daisies and other field flowers bent with the breeze in a constantly moving mixture of summer colours.

Here and there, in the patchwork of fields on the other side of the river, men and machines dwarfed by the distance began to work at one or another of the various stages of making hay. White, fine-weather clouds, drifting high overhead, cast occasional shadows on the fields and hills, and seemed to be present both above and below us as their mirrored reflections slipped downriver among the upside-down spruces and firs and bankside hardwoods.

It didn't take too long for us to pick a dozen boxes or so and we left the field with red stained fingers and a strawberry taste on our lips, for if you pick a berry that's too ripe to keep but too good to waste there's only one sensible thing to do with it. Most of the berries picked that morning were boiled up with sugar on the old wood stove and ended up as bottles of jam on the kitchen table. So that, in the course of time, we enjoyed some pleasant memories of a summer morning with our January breakfasts.

A Birthday For Mrs. Clarke

1979

In the George Frederick Clarke house in Woodstock, family birthdays have always been looked upon as special occasions. At dinner time in the panelled dining room, the long mahogany table under the glittering chandelier is set with goblet and silver and fine china, with a centrepiece of seasonal flowers. The climax of a fine meal is the entrance of the candle-studded cake and the singing of the traditional "Happy Birthday" song, sometimes in a variety of keys but always with gusto. And then there's a present-opening sequel. The atmosphere is such that I'm sure old Father Time himself must be repeatedly pleased with the relaxed formality of these recognitions of his existence.

This year, a very special birthday celebration recognizes the fact that the lady who presides at the table, and set the tone for these regular occasions, is herself 90 years of age. Mary Schubert Clarke was born on August 10th, 1889 in Philadelphia, where she lived until her marriage to the young dentist and aspiring author Dr. George Frederick Clarke of Woodstock, NB.

My first sight of Mrs. Clarke, who has been my mother-in-law for nearly forty years, was at a reception and dance held at Mount Allison University during my post-graduate year. She wore a long evening dress, and her wide blue eyes and radiant smile created an aura of whole-hearted friendliness mingled with a touch of the kind of reserve one associates with royalty. When her daughter Dees introduced me to her, I remember thinking that she was one of the most beautiful ladies I had ever met. When I became a member of the family and grew to be familiar with the red brick house on upper Main St., I realized how much its furnishing reflected a combination of Mrs. Clarke's own good taste and the many interests of her energetic husband, for example his passion for acquiring and restoring fine pieces of antique furniture.

Family photograph albums, inscribed volumes, and my own summer experiences revealed the extent and variety of Mrs. Clarke's responsibilities as hostess over the years. There were guests from the world of Canadian literature — Bliss Carman, Sir Charles G.D. Roberts, Wilson MacDonald[53] — and editors of national magazines or publishers' representatives. Then there were archaeologists from American universities and museums who wanted to talk to Dr. Clarke about his extensive collection of Indian artifacts, acquired through many years of constant searching over ploughed fields or ancient campsites.

There were old mutual friends from Philadelphia, the New England States, and cities in Canada. Many members of the salmon angling fraternity who read Dr. Clarke's *Six Salmon Rivers and Another* and *The Song of the Reel* wanted to meet the author who, as they said, "Could take them back to the river at a turn of the page." They would come to call on their way to the Restigouche or the Miramichi; American millionaires, Montreal businessmen, fisherman from all walks of life. And there were children who came to hear Dr. Clarke talk about the early days in Acadia or to gather material for history assignments.

Mrs. Clarke was never self-effacing, but she seemed to know instinctively when to stay in the living room and when she could slip away in pursuit of some of her own interests (her reading or painting or gardening) until it was time to produce the leaden tray with ingredients for a nice cup of tea and something to go with it. She has always been concerned about material comforts of anyone for whom she feels responsible, temporarily or permanently. In the dedication of *The Song of the Reel*, Dr. Clarke wrote: "To My Wife, who for fifty summers has helped pack my dunnage, and not forgetting the smallest necessity, sent me off to the rivers or the woods with the cheery words: 'Have a good time. Take care of yourself. Good luck.'"

53 Bliss Carman (1861-1929), Charles G.D. Roberts (1860-1943), and Wilson MacDonald (1880-1967) were Canadian poets. Carman and Roberts were cousins, born in New Brunswick and, along with Archibald Lampman (1861-99) and Duncan Campbell Scott (1862-1947), were among the first critically-acclaimed poets following the birth of Canada and hence became known as the "Confederation Poets."

When Dees and I were living in Montreal, Mrs. Clarke would sometimes send us parcels of homemade bread and cookies and other good things. Once, I remember during war times, and this is illustrative of her optimistic belief that good intentions are their own safeguard, she sent us, through the mail, a pound of Carleton County butter with no protection except the brown paper wrapper in which it came from the store, and it arrived intact, with scarcely a dent in it.

Mrs. Clarke was always active in the social and service life of her community, and one of her most regretted concessions to the passage of time, and a series of operations, was giving up driving the car. One summer day about three years ago, when she was convalescing after having fallen and broken a leg, and undergoing an operation for her arthritic knee, Dees and I encountered her in the back yard with one hand behind her back and a mischievous look in her eye. "I was just going to see," she said, "if I could get into the driver's seat." With some difficulty she managed it, started the car and drove 'round the house. Dees and I went around the other way to help her out, if need be, only to catch a glimpse of the twilight as the car turned onto the highway and off for a jaunt of a few miles into the county. Mrs. Clarke drove back wearing the impish expression of a young truant who had skipped school on a sunny afternoon and was completely unrepentant about it. But she did agree in future to accept the doctor's dictum.

Mrs. Clarke is still an active member of the community, attending St Luke's Anglican Church each Sunday morning, meetings of the Carleton County Historical Society, and the I.O.D.E.[54] She enjoys travelling. On July 7, 1977 she went to England with her daughter Jane, and this spring she flew on her own to Montreal to spend a week with Jane. And she continues to maintain a lively motherly, grandmotherly, and great-grandmotherly interest in the doings and accomplishments and sayings of her children, her grandchildren, and her great-grandchildren.

She still gives personal attention to her beloved roses, cane in one hand and a bottle of rose food in the other, and her cookbooks

54 Imperial Order Daughters of the Empire, founded in 1900 in Fredericton, NB, is a charitable organization which remains active in Canada today focusing on children, education, and community services

are still in constant use. I'm sure she greets with semi-indignant questioning my occasional fraternal suggestions that she shouldn't try to do everything she used to do, such as going upstairs with one hand holding up her dressing gown and with a pile of sheets over the arm that should be concentrated on the railing.

But be that as it may, I can see that in this 90th birthday week there are scores of well-wishers in many communities in New Brunswick and abroad who hope that she will long continue to preside over the teacups in the red brick house with the pillars on upper Main St. in Woodstock, a house that so uniquely continues to reflect the combined personalities of Dr. George Frederick Clarke and his "dear wife" Mary.

An Evening By The River

1978

Much has been written about the fact that bodies of water large and small have an undeniable fascination for members of the human race. From wind-riffled rain puddles to the great salt seas, they affect the eye and stimulate the mind. I can remember, as a boy, watching for hours the long green combers roll in from the Atlantic, so that when I went to bed at night the waves kept breaking behind my closed eyelids. And there were trout streams gurgling and rippling over golden gravel through the forest, with pockets of foam caught in the branches of fallen trees, and intermittent pools where the shadows of invisible fishes darted along the sloping sides toward the obscurity of darkened depths.

And then there were larger rivers to carry a canoe, now smoothly and steadily over deep water, and again precipitately, in the heady tumult of white rapids that called for skill with pole or paddle. Then there were lakes, large and small, each with associations and memories recalled instantly by the sound of water lapping over sand or shingle. And all of these, in and around, above and below, are so teeming with life, finned, furred, and feathered, or borne in stem, leaf and blossom, vital products of their separate and special environments.

Last evening, after supper, I sat under a maple tree by the bank of the river and smoked my pipe and just watched. The scene was drenched with August sunlight still, though the sun was near the point where we lose it behind our high western hillside. The water was calm except for small squally patches here and there, where vagrant light winds collided over the surface. Elsewhere, a round of ripples started whenever a small fish made its brief silver appearance and plopped back down again, or when the wing tip of a diving swallow touched the surface as it wheeled in pursuit of an elusive fly.

From the far side of the river came a single distinctive call identifying the pair of loons drifting down over the shimmering reflection of Sharp's Mountain. In a little while, a moving speck in the southern sky became large enough to be recognized as our resident osprey who paused and circled and dropped like a stone into the water, apparently without success. But, seconds after he mounted into the air, he dropped again and then emerged in a shower of spray to fly with a fish to the bare branch of a dead tree on the hillside. Down along the shore, a procession of nearly grown young ducks appeared briefly and then disappeared from sight behind the tangle of vegetation, a veritable curtain of berry canes, wild grape vines, and multifarious weeds and flowers. A solitary tern flew out over the river and set off downstream, making me wonder why we had seen so little of the sea-birds this summer, the herring gulls and black-backed gulls that usually keep us mindful of the sea's presence at the river's end.

As the sun dipped behind the western hill, and the light moved across the river, the little fish redoubled their leaping efforts, and round ripples ran into one another on the darkling surface of the shadowed water. My wife, who had come to join me, said quietly, "Look, Ken," and a great blue heron swept past so close to the bank that we could hear the rhythmic susurration of its wide wings. A flock of red-winged blackbirds rose from the cattails by the pond and flew out over the river into the sunlight, their congregation signalling the imminent ending of the summer season. When the creeping shadows reached the mountain's base, they climbed quite quickly up the wooded slope, and after a final burst of gold intensity, the light began to fade. A little later, the dark water would mirror the stars, except in the path of light from the late rising moon.

Sometimes I wonder whether, in these seaside provinces, with our lakes and streams and rivers near at hand, we fully realize how fortunate we have been. We should not need the impassioned prose of a Herman Melville or the nostalgic reminiscences of a Mark Twain, only the evidence of our five senses. And we need to remember, too, that each of us bears a responsibility to protect our heritage for future generations.

Francis Peabody Sharp

1976

Whenever I drive up through Upper Woodstock at sunset time, my eyes are usually turned somewhat to the left to catch the colours of the western sky. Always I come to the place where I notice, on the gently rising slope of a field behind the houses, a large stand of apple trees silhouetted against the last light of the day. And often I think of the man under whose direction they were planted before the turn of the century.

New Brunswick's pioneer horticulturist, Francis Peabody Sharp, was born in Carleton County in 1823. He was scientifically inclined from an early age and he hoped to follow a career in medicine; but he was advised, for reasons of health, to choose an occupation which would keep him out of doors. The young man was familiar with growing things through boyhood work in his father's garden and orchard, so he decided to exercise his scientific bent in the direction of developing varieties of fruit trees that would make possible commercial horticulture in the cold climate of New Brunswick. The importance to New Brunswick of his research over the next half century can be compared to that of Luther Burbank[55] for California, and Sharp began his work a good many years before that of the famous American.

Through scientific selection and hybridization, Sharp produced a number of new apple varieties, including the well-known New Brunswicker and Crimson Beauty.[56] He established a commercial nursery in 1844 and later expanded it in partnership with his brother-in-law, Sperry Shea, in 1870. As time went on, the Sharp and Shea

---

55 Luther Burbank (1849 - 1926), American botanist, horticulturist, and a pioneer in agricultural science. He developed numerous strains and varieties of plants including the Shasta Daisy and the Burbank potato, precursor to the Russet Burbank.

56 Both varieties remain available today, in New Brunswick and Maine, in limited production.

Nurseries supplied scores of orchards in New Brunswick and the northern United States with trees suited for commercial use under our severe climatic conditions.

Sharp's experiments were not limited to apple growing, as he tried to develop suitable varieties of other fruit as well, particularly pears and plums. It was almost by accident that he discovered a method of increasing yield and speeding up the fruiting of plum trees. One of his young trees had been bent over in a winter storm and buried under a snowdrift until spring came. Sharp observed that this tree fruited much sooner than might have been expected under normal conditions. As an experiment, he bent over and fastened down a number of trees the next autumn and they, too, followed the pattern of the accidental example of the winter before, a discovery of great importance in the field of plum culture.

In addition to the creation of new apple varieties, Francis Peabody Sharp also recommended innovations in planting and cultivation practices, placing his trees much closer together in the row than those of other orchards. Throughout his career as nurseryman and orchardist, he maintained experimental plots and kept meticulous records of successes and failures. Most of the profits from his enterprises went back into experimental work and, when the orchard industry here was hit hard by high American import tariffs, there were financial difficulties. Sharp handed his business to his son, Franklin, in 1887, but unfortunately the son died in 1892, and attempts by other members of the family to keep going were unsuccessful. The orchards were sold in 1904, and the Nova Scotian who bought them chopped out the experimental plots.

Edwin Tappan Adney, who married one of Sharp's daughters, wrote about the accomplishments of his father-in-law. Among other things, Adney told of Francis Peabody Sharp's successful experiments dealing with fruition control in conformity with what he called "the law of antagonism between stalk and fruit." Adney wrote in 1911, and I quote,

> All previously known methods of inducing fruition, as root-pruning, led only to diminished capacity, while Sharp's method, on the contrary, invited a root system

> of utmost capacity. The only result was a dwarfing of the tree, and a tree could be made to bear at any age. He had a plum tree six inches high with a plum on it. He put nursery trees three feet high into heavy bearing, and even accomplished the astonishing feat of producing an apple sixteen months from seed.
>
> Not only did he turn leaf buds into fruit buds, but what is still more marvelous, reversed the process and caused fruit buds to make a stalk instead of fruit. Wonderful are some of the results of cross fertilizing, but more truly wonderful are some of these accomplishments of Sharp's.

An interesting point about all this is the present day field workers of the Provincial Horticultural Branch of the Department of Agriculture are advocating the adoption of many of the methods and practices recommended by Francis Peabody Sharp over a hundred years ago.

Francis Peabody Sharp died of pneumonia in December, 1903. A few years ago I talked with a lady who remembered seeing him as an old man, his long white beard waving in the late autumn wind, working with an experimental plot of onions at Grafton on the bank of the St. John River opposite Upper Woodstock. This was shortly before he died, a scientific observer to the very end of his life. I continue to be impressed by the magnitude of his accomplishments and somewhat concerned that they have received so little official recognition, his only memorial being the remnant of what was once the largest orchard in the Maritimes standing out against the western sky at sunset time.

Autumn

The Quality Of Autumn Light

1979

Each year, when mid-September comes around, there are certain times of day when changes in the quality of light itself prophesy autumn's imminent arrival, as surely as the turning of the leaves. And each year about this time, the thought comes to me that if I were an artist, I would be working intensively, dawn to dusk, from now until the falling of the snow. In late September there is such variety, the more noticeable since the sun rises at a reasonable hour, and we're conscious of the whole range of rich illumination from early morning until sunset.

The other day, beyond the morning mist, I watched the glow of eastern light intensify until, suddenly, white clouds drifted high above the river and the hills changed to a roseate pink, which spread and deepened as darker clouds caught the moving colour, and half of the sky was aflame. At high noon on that same day, a pair of vagrant winds contended for direction over the river's surface and the sun, as bright as in mid-July, struck so many points of flashing brilliance from the water that I had to slit my eyes. And that day, as the afternoon wore on, the sunlight, without relinquishing any of its summer warmth, assumed a mellow, golden quality, a foretaste of that peculiar radiance which is one of autumn's chief glories, a light which transforms familiar landscapes, blunting sharp images and softening contours, working in subtle partnership with shadows to recreate the natural world.

Occasionally now, the tattered remnants of tropical storms send banks of dark clouds moving up the river just as, soon, the northwest winds will send them moving down. In both cases the sun, shining through blue rents in the morning vapour, will touch the hills here and there with a brightness that irresistibly attracts the eye to the surviving green or autumn colours of forest trees, and to the gilded stubble fields of hillside farms, until the light moves on or fades to shadow as the cloud rents close.

I have heard summer visitors from European countries speak of the hardness or harshness of our North American light, but I am certain that if they were to observe it through all seasons they would find it as variable as sunlight anywhere on earth. There are many people in this province of New Brunswick who would say that they are too busy to notice such relatively unimportant things, and this applies not only to those who spend their days in city offices but also to those whose responsibility it is to bring in the harvest of the summer's growing. The world around them gets only peripheral attention as eyes focus constantly on the requirements of the matter in hand.

There is something sad about this, since we have so little time under the sun, and the sun of our individual autumns is so pitifully small. There is so much to see for those who look at any season of the turning year, but when it comes to appreciation of the very light which brings the objects to our eyes, the next few weeks will provide such subtle changes and such varied pleasure that I, for one, become especially grateful for the gift of sight.

Ancient Harvest Myths

1977

In this time of harvest, men and women give thanks for the bounties of the land as they have done through time immemorial. It is little wonder that the ancients deified the power that mysteriously brought forth grain from seed, or that the legends of the goddess date back some 9,000 years. In ancient Greece she was known as Demeter, daughter of Cronos and Rhea, the oldest of the Olympian band who had also given birth to the great Zeus. The women of those days who worked the land, seeding it and reaping the resultant harvest, considered every chore that helped to make the farm fruitful an act of worship, more pleasing to the Earth Mother than the bloody sacrifices offered to other gods.

Once every five years, in the months of September, a nine-day festival was held in her honour, with parades and spectacles, dance and song. In later years were added secret celebrations, of which Cicero said in Roman times, "They have sweetened our characters and softened our customs; they have made us pass from the condition of savages to true humanity. They have not only shown us the way to live joyfully, but they have taught us how to die with a better hope."[57]

Believing implicitly in the goodness and generosity of the Earth goddess, the ancients wondered why a part of the year should be unfruitful and uncomfortable, shorn of the green and growing things in the cold dark days of the winter months. And for this, their legends also gave an explanation.

Demeter had an only daughter, Persephone, as lovely as the springtime itself. The Lord of the Underworld,[58] having seen her, was

57 Cicero (106-43) regarding the Eleusinian Mysteries, ancient Greek and Roman religious rituals inspired by the myth of Demeter.

58 In Greek mythology, Hades is the ruler of the dead. A child of Cronos and Rhea, his siblings include Zeus and Demeter, making him an uncle to Persephone.

determined to have her as his queen. One day, when she was out walking with her youthful companions, Persephone wandered away from them in search of flowers, and the king of the dead perceived his chance. His chariot carried him up through a dark chasm from his shadowy realm into the bright sunlight. Reining in his coal-black steeds he leaped from his chariot, seized the frightened maid, and seated her beside him. Then back he dove, down and down into the bowels of the earth, to his underworld kingdom.

When Demeter discovered that her daughter was missing, she searched for her, over the sea and over the land throughout the world, without success. At last, she learned that Persephone was no longer upon earth, but one among the multitudes in the realm of the ghostly dead. Her grief knew no bounds, and under its spell she neglected her divine duties. Nothing would grow. No seeds sprang into life, and the green leaves withered and fell to the barren ground. She was deaf to the pleas and prayers of alarmed mankind, who feared that death by famine would eliminate the human race.

But if Demeter seemed deaf to the imploring cries, Zeus heard. He sent one after another of the Olympians to Demeter to speak to her on man's behalf, but they were unable to move her. Then he sent his messenger Hermes down the steep passages and over the mysterious River Styx, to meet with the Lord of the Underworld and to arrange with him a compromise concerning the disposition of his beautiful bride. Also he dispatched old Rhea to tell Demeter that her daughter would be restored to her for two-thirds of each year. The other four months she would spend with her dark consort in the realm of the dead. All this upon condition that Demeter would once more provide for the welfare of the blasted world.

So Demeter, overjoyed, relented and set about restoring the earth which, by her neglect, had been left desolate. Now, once again, the green leaves grew on the rustling branches, the wind ran in waves through the growing grasses, and the seeds of the sowers bore fair and fruitfully. All was as it had been in the days before the abduction of Persephone, except that during the four months of each year when she was separated from her mother, the earth shared Demeter's grief and ceased to bear, displaying instead a winter aspect of sympathetic sorrow. But men and women no longer despaired, knowing that the time would pass and the spring would come again with Persephone's annual release, and there would be a return of life and beauty to the withered land.

A modern meteorologist would consider this a somewhat naïve explanation for the changing seasons, but there still remains in the minds of most men a sense of wonder concerning the mysteries of life and growth, and we share an unspoken kinship with those who gave thanks for the harvest so many centuries ago.

Frolicking Ravens & Other Birds

1976

One day earlier this month, a warm south wind came moving up the St. John River valley, wrinkling the reflections in the pond near our house, and causing sporadic showers of butternut leaves, which are always among the first to fall. The way some of them whirled high into the air before drifting down to the ground, or over the water, gave evidence of rising thermals, and there was a further indication of their presence when my wife called me to come and watch the ravens.

About a dozen of the black birds were riding the wind high above the hillside woods and putting on a performance I'll not soon forget. With hardly any movement of their wings, they soared singly or in groups, rising higher and higher until, all at once, some of them would slice downward through the air in graceful arcs. Others, with half-folded pinions, would come tumbling hundreds of feet down the sky to end their fall with a sideline sweep over the treetops before the rising wind carried them aloft again. Sometimes, three or four of them would break away from the main group in a remarkable example of precision gliding, turning as one, this way or that, upwards or downwards, as though connected by some invisible bond.

Occasionally, the whole group would be wheeling about in a realistic imitation of aerial combat, a dogfight situation with each bird attempting to secure an attack position above the back of another. And sometimes some of them even seemed to be playing a peculiar game of tag, with one raven swooping beneath another and then turning upside down to push with his feet against the feet of the one above. The lower bird would fall away with a flutter of wings before catching the rising current and soaring upwards once again.

The ravens kept up their performance against the background of white clouds and the blue sky between for quite some time, and then sped off along the tree line, croaking or uttering a deep-throated rattling sound as they flew by. As far as I could tell, there seemed to be no particular reason or purpose behind the display of aerobatics, except that of sheer enjoyment. The birds seemed to be playing in the warm air currents with all the carefree abandon of children in an old swimming hole.

September is an interesting month for bird watchers. So many species gather in flocks at this time of year and appear to be in training for the long migration flights that soon will come. By now, some of the song birds have already gone, but the red-winged blackbirds, for example, still rise each morning from among the cattails by the thousands, flying in tight groups of a couple of hundred or so up the river and down, returning to roost at nightfall, bending the cattail stalks with the weight of their numbers. There are times when the slender branches of the small willow trees in our old back garden are festooned with the chattering tribe, a black decoration interspersed with flashing touches of scarlet as wings flutter in restless motion. A sudden movement by the dog, or one of the cats, will send them off again, rising in unison to fly overhead with a distinct whistle of a thousand wings. This is the time, too, when you're apt to see scores of cedar waxwings gobbling the scarlet berries of the mountain ash, regardless of the danger of intoxication that sometimes follows a surfeit of such food — another example of autumn group activity.

In the past two decades, more and more people have become active observers of birds and their habits. There is a growing realization of the tremendous contribution made by these winged participants in the scheme of things, far outweighing any problems they might cause. Publicity given threatened species now arouses a more informed public opinion, which is beginning to make itself felt in influencing the conduct of spray programs and other environmental threats to the continued existence of a healthy feathered population. If the trend continues at the present rate, we may someday be assured that no quiet winter will ever be followed by a silent spring.[59]

---

59 Likely an acknowledgement of the work of Rachel Carson (1907-64), American conservationist and author of *Silent Spring*, which described the harmful effects of pesticides on the environment.

Butternuts

1976

All during the autumn days until very recently, at any time of the day or night at our house by the St. John River, you'd be apt to hear a peculiar sound on the roof that went "thump... clump... rattle, rattle, rattle," and ended with a light "plop" on the ground outside. At first, Princess would bark every time she heard it, but finally she got used to it and paid as little attention as if she knew it was just another butternut that had slipped its moorings. The old butternut tree at the front corner of our house had a bumper crop this year, and enough of the noisy green projectiles rolled down the roof to practically cobble the ground below.

Butternut trees, I've discovered, are members of the walnut family and sometimes are referred to as white walnut. They're pretty well restricted to the St. John River Valley in this province. We know that the wood of the butternut tree is a favourite of cabinet makers for certain specific purposes and that the meat of the nut has a subtle flavour all its own, more delicate than that of other walnuts. The pioneers of this part of the world made good use of it in the preparation of some of the cakes and cookies that somehow were included in the era of fireplace cookery. The ladies, too, in their search for dyes to lend colour to the products of their looms, found in the butternut coating a rich source of natural pigment, a sort of brownish gold in colour, and that's understandable to anyone who looks at his stained fingers after handling a few of the sticky clusters.

There is one drawback to the enjoyment of the butternut and that is it's a very hard nut to crack. I suggest that one of the reasons for the success in life secured by many St. John River Valley men is that the task of cracking butternuts for their mothers' pantries in their younger days taught them perseverance and patience. It took much practice to develop the skill required to break the ribbed, brown, inner nut in such a way as to extract the kernels without crushing them.

Two years ago, in the last autumn of his long life, my late father-in-law, Dr. George Frederick Clarke, sat in a camp chair at the side of the pond near our house, feasting his eyes on the fall colours of the hillside hardwood trees which were almost unbelievable in their brilliance. As he finally rose and walked toward the house with my wife, Dees, he looked down at the ground and said, "Dees, fetch me a hammer." While Dees went to get the hammer and a piece of slate rock from the river bank, Dr. Clarke collected a baker's dozen of plump butternuts. Then, sitting down slowly on the front step, he swung his legs carefully around to the side until he was in a comfortable position. He took the hammer in one hand and, with the other, held one of the oblong nuts upright on the piece of rock. Knowing how difficult the job was, Dees was a bit concerned about his ability to crack it, but she needn't have worried. With unerring skill, Dr. Clarke proceeded to crack them all, sharing the sweet kernels with his admiring daughter. Only someone who has made the effort will realize that this was quite an accomplishment for a man in his 91st year.

For some reason or other, one rarely sees a grove of butternut trees. They are more likely to appear here and there in conjunction with other hardwoods. This seeming reluctance to share the company of their own kind, plus the unpredictability of yield in any one year, and the difficulty of extracting the kernels, all mitigate against the possibility of commercial production. But many inhabitants of the St. John River Valley, even in this day and age, would no more neglect the garnering of a good store of butternuts than they would overlook the picking of fiddleheads in the spring. I would wager that in many a rural attic right now there's a floor-wide layer of green-coated butternuts gradually drying to a crisp brown against the time of their welcome contribution to the Christmas cooking.

Attic Distractions

1980

The other day, my wife Dees and I were moving things about in the attic of the G.F. Clarke house in Woodstock so that the insulators could have room to perform their energy-saving function. Among those things were baskets and boxes containing stone age Indian artifacts, spillovers from Dr. Clarke's collection of Maliseet implements of war and chase and everyday life along the banks of rivers that were Indian highways. There were sledges and axes and scrapers; knives and spearheads and arrowheads, some whole, some broken; and there were pottery shards and chippings of various kinds and colours — the result of many hours of patient searching on banks and intervales of the St. John, the Tobique and the Miramichi.

In memory, I could clearly see Dr. Clarke's erect figure, clad in tweed and corduroy, the brim of his felt hat at a jaunty angle, pipe clenched between his teeth, striding along the furrows of ploughed fields in fall or spring. Occasionally, he'd pause to turn over a stone with the tip of the cane he carried, and I remember that if he stooped to pick up something, I would pause in my own searching to see whether he would cast it aside or put it in his pocket. For there is a sense of excitement in finding these traces of older civilization, in the realization that 500, 1,000 or perhaps 2,000 years ago, a pair of human hands fashioned the objects that the actions of frost and the plough were returning to the light of day. I remembered, too, that Sheila Burnford[60] in one of the essays which make up her book, *The Fields of Noon*, had described her ventures as an amateur archaeologist and had defined and explored this feeling of excitement most admirably. When the last of the cartons, et cetera, in the attic had been suitably

60 Sheila Burnford (1918-84), British-born Canadian author who also wrote *The Incredible Journey*, (1961) the story of three pets travelling through the Canadian wilderness in search of their masters, which was made (and re-made) into a Disney movie.

shifted, I went to look for *The Fields of Noon* in various bookcases all over the house.

Now, whenever I stand with shelves of books in front of me, I can't resist turning a cover or two, and soon I was reading some of the letters Dorothy Osborne wrote to Sir William Temple over a seven-year period in the troubled times of pre-Restoration England.[61] Just before the marriage of these two was eventually scheduled to take place, the elements of tragedy arose when mistress Osborne fell ill of smallpox. It did not take her life, but it blemished her beauty. Sir William, however, gallantly married her just the same and they seem to have enjoyed a most satisfactory relationship over the next forty years or so.

Realizing that this was not the time to lose myself in the social life of the 17th century, I continued my search, but soon found myself with another open book in my hands. It was the book of Epictetus, the lame slave who became a noted Greek philosopher and some of whose discourses, preserved by one of his disciples, have come down to us as the major source of information concerning the nature of stoic philosophy. As the editor of this volume said of Epictetus:

> What he saw, he saw intensely and recorded with power and fidelity. And he saw much that we would be well to see with him. He sent a piercing beam of light into the recesses of the human soul, and he discovered there the unconquerable will, the capacity for spiritual freedom, to which in times of perplexity and discouragement troubled souls have always turned as to the sheet-anchor of their moral life.

And so there I was beginning to read such bits of philosophic advice as:

> Remember that you are an actor in a drama, of such a kind as the author pleases to make it. If short, a short

61 *The Love Letters of Dorothy Osborne to Sir William Temple* were first published in 1888, edited by E.A Parry.

> one; if long, a long one. If it be his pleasure you should act a poor man, a cripple, a governor, or a private person, see that you act it naturally. For this is your business, to act well the character assigned you; to choose it is another's.[62]

My next distraction was in the stylistically colourful fictional prose of James Branch Cabell[63] whose book, *Chivalry,* fell open at the story which describes the death of Richard II in Pontefract Castle in 1400 — only in this case the victim is portrayed as being Richard's older brother Edward who, the story goes, had taken the place and suffered the fate of the real king.

So I have not yet found *The Fields of Noon,* and the passage which I had hoped to read for you, describing so well the excitement engendered by tangible communication with the remote past, will have to wait another time.

62 Epictetus, *The Enchiridion*, Part 17, c. AD 135

63 James Branch Cabell (1879-1958), American author of fantasy fiction.

The Springhill Disaster

1978

This week marks the 20th anniversary of the mining disaster at Springhill, Nova Scotia. Seventy-five of 174 men in the Cumberland mine lost their lives as the result of a "bump" or sudden shifting of subterranean pressure that occurred on October 23, 1958. I was part of the CBC crew which covered the disaster, and yesterday I searched out a file which contained a few scribbled reports and lifted one out at random. We had little time to write anything down at the height of the action, but this account had been given about four days after the bump. Eighty-one men had been taken alive from the mine. There were still 93 either dead or missing and hope for further rescue had just about been abandoned. The night I read the following was one of the few times that dismal week the rain had stopped falling. This is what I said:

> Things are quiet in Springhill. There is little movement around the pithead, except for the occasional comings and goings of police vehicles and the periodic single-file of a draegerman rescue crew leaving or entering the mine. It's a bright clear moonlit night and the long metal-walled bankhead building gleams in the background of the mineyard, behind the line of waiting ambulances. Newsmen are taking a well-deserved rest, after the days' round of interviews and press conferences. The television cameras have stopped grinding. And most of the youngsters who clustered around the monitor screens have been taken home to bed. Below ground, the working crew continues its slow laborious progress through fallen rock and timbers toward the 13,000 foot level. In the warmth of the washhouse, the miners still cluster in small groups, sharing opinions about the cause

> of the disaster and questioning those who are cleaning off the dust and grime of a completed shift below.
>
> In spite of repeated assurances that no developments are expected during the night, there are still relatives and friends in the area behind the restraining ropes near the pithead entrance sharing with one another the watchful waiting which began shortly after 8 o'clock on Thursday, and which will continue until all the miners have been accounted for. In the town itself, lights are burning in nearly every dwelling. A dark house usually means that neighbours are visiting neighbours, seeking the comfort of a friendly pot of tea or coffee. The dim glimmer of hope that there may be living men in the bump area is seldom referred to now, but it still may be seen in the reddening eyes of Springhill residents who have become strangers to sleep. I might have said, simply, that there is nothing to report from Springhill, but even though repetition and the lengthening hours have dulled the impact of the tragic drama being enacted here, it will not come to an end until the work below is finished, and the waiting relatives receive the final answer to their unspoken questions.

I remember well the despondency and despair of the next few rainy days; the official announcement that the company did not expect to find further life in the black depths; the funerals; the desertion of the site by press, radio, and television crews who thought the sad story was ready for the traditional "30."[64]

Then on Wednesday, October 29th, came the electrifying news that a pocket had been discovered at the 13,000 foot level containing 12 men who were still alive. Since I was the only broadcaster left on the

---

64 "-30-" was used by journalists to indicate the end of a story. It was one of many abbreviations standardized as part of the "Phillips Code" created in 1879 by Walter Phillips for the Associated Press for transmission of press reports by telegraph.

scene, I suppose I have never before or since had a greater audience, for half the world had been following the events at Springhill. In a few hours, reporters and commentators came flooding back to cover the rescue and an informal visit by His Royal Highness, Prince Philip. There was further great rejoicing on Saturday morning, when seven more living miners were found.[65]

But a great tragedy had occurred and, in looking back on it, I can say that never have I been more aware of the untapped reserves of strength and courage in the human race. They were evident in the gallant stoicism of the families waiting at the pithead; they kept 19 men alive during dark days of apparent hopelessness; they tripled the progress of rescuers through solid walls of coal and rock when it became known that life lay beyond; and they helped the people of a stricken community to carry on in spite of disaster.

65 Although 100 miners were taken from the mine alive, one died later in hospital, raising the death toll to 75.

Baked Beans & Other Culinary Matters

1978

One Saturday evening recently, a young friend of ours, David Bell, asked me if, when I was young, we always had baked beans for supper on Saturday nights. As I recall, the hearty one-dish meal did appear with weekly regularity accompanied by the traditional loaf of homemade brown bread, and this was true in the homes of most of my friends and neighbours in the Nova Scotia town where I was born. David, who is blessed with an inquisitive mind and a great sense of history, wanted to know why, and there wasn't much that I could tell him that wasn't pure speculation on my part.

It is a matter of history that the Indians were using what the Americans later came to call "navy" beans when the Pilgrims and Puritans came, and it's reasonable to assume that the new arrivals adopted this as one of their staple foods. How, and at what point, the combination of beans with pork and onions, mustard and molasses came into being, I do not know. Dees checked some of her recipe books and it appears that the product known as "Boston" baked beans invariably called for molasses, where some of the others used brown sugar as a replacement. Our area in southwest Nova Scotia was settled by the planters who came there from Massachusetts in the 1760s, at the invitation of Governor Lawrence, a few years after the expulsion of the Acadians. Undoubtedly, these New Englanders brought their appetite for baked beans with them, as did their contemporaries to other parts of the Maritimes.

Now, why Saturday night? In the olden days, Saturday was the time where families in rural areas took a bath, got slicked up, and went to the nearest settlement for market day. When the wagon or carriage rattled home again at the end of the day, how easy it would be for the lady of the house to warm up a pot of pre-prepared beans while the menfolk were getting the chores done. In any case, whether for some such reason as this or by arbitrary choice, Saturday night has been bean night in many Maritime families for over two centuries.

Nowadays, a pot with some leftover beans in it is a good thing to have around against the increasingly numerous occasions when a man finds it necessary to fend for himself at supper time. Once, you know, a man would consider that he had lost face if he admitted that he knew how to boil an egg. That sort of thing was strictly woman's work and very much beneath his dignity. Now, you'll even find some who are proud of the fact that they can quite easily cope with a meal-getting situation, and that doesn't mean simply slipping a frozen TV dinner into the oven to heat up.

In my own case, I find that one way over the hurdle is to check the refrigerator for leftovers. Last night for example, I knew that Dees was going to be late coming up from her mother's, so I decided to get the supper ready myself. My foraging survey was very productive — there were some mashed potatoes, a few boiled onions in a butter sauce, and a carton of cream-style corn in the fridge. Also, there were some meatballs in a gourmet gravy leftover from one of our recent meals. I sliced some bits of onion over some butter in a frying pan and when they became transparent I added the mashed potatoes. The corn and the boiled onions and the meatballs went into iron saucepans for almost instant heating on the old kitchen stove. I opened a can of peach halves, cut the halves into bits, sliced in a couple of bananas and some maraschino cherries for flavour and eye appeal, and that made an easy dessert. So, thanks to the refrigerator, I was able to produce a very acceptable meal in about 15 minutes.

It's easy for a man to build himself a reputation as a cook if he makes himself proficient in the preparation of one or two tasty meals. I came across a recipe for such a meal in a book on southern cooking, and I've produced it to resounding applause on one or two occasions in the past. If you would like to try it you'll need some pork chops cut generously thick, some sweet potatoes, some apples, and some raisins. In advance, boil a few regular potatoes and prepare a dressing with onions, summer savory, and the rest of it, just as you would for stuffing poultry. Parboil the sweet potatoes and lightly season the pork chops. Then you get a roasting pan, place the pork chops in it, each surmounted by a mound of dressing, add the sweet potatoes, core some large apples and put them in too, filling the holes with raisins. Then bake in the covered pan until the meat is done. You'll find the blended flavours of the separate ingredients a very convincing argument on which to build a gourmet reputation.

Homemade Bread

1977

One day not long ago when I went into my mother-in-law's house, there was a most delectable fragrance drifting through the air from the kitchen. I was just in time to watch the last of a number of loaves of homemade bread come out of the oven. It wasn't long before my sense of taste verified the message of the olfactory introduction. I maintain, with all due respect to the excellent bakeries which supply most of us with our daily ration of the staff of life, that there is nothing that can compare with the flavour, texture, and aroma of bread that's baked at home and sampled soon after it's out of the pan.

Over the years, I have been fortunate enough to enjoy the hospitality of country homes and farm kitchens in all three Maritime provinces, and one of the things that has made these occasions memorable is the quality of the homemade bread. When I was a boy, my mother used to bake bread sometimes, and it was considered to be a regular treat in our house as long as it lasted, which wasn't very long. During my days at university, I would sometimes get a parcel from home, containing among other things: a cooked tongue, some pickles, and a loaf of brown oatmeal bread. The word soon went 'round. Someone would "borrow" a pat of butter from the dining hall, someone else would filch a pitcher of milk, and that night, a few of us would temporarily satisfy our mutual longing for home cooking. "Tell your mother," one of them would say with a flourish, "that Olympian ambrosia pales to a poor second compared to her beneficent bounty."

In my late teens, I spent a number of summers as a counsellor at a boy's camp. The cook was a man of Acadian ancestry who did all his own baking. I can see him now on a hot July day, dressed only in khaki shorts under his long white apron, kneading a massive pile of dough in the camp kitchen while a wood fire crackled in the big galley stove.

Sweat glistened on his forehead and his strong arms, and he'd say with a grin, "That's what gives my bread its special flavour!"

In those days, you used to be able to go to the drug store and buy the ingredients for homemade root beer. You would mix sugar and water in a big tub, add the drug store ingredients, and bottle the result. One of the other camp counsellors would bring a few jugs of root beer with him when he came to camp and there would always be one on the end of a long rope hanging down the well. After the boys were asleep in their tents, we counsellors would gravitate to the kitchen. We'd pull up the jug, get out the breadknife, and soon we'd be enjoying a cold drink along with hearty slices of Harvey's homemade bread, generously topped with country butter.

The very thought of it brings back the memory of those summer nights, with a full moon riding high over the lake, crickets singing in the campus grass, the air cooled and sweet after shedding its burden of the day's hot sunshine and, with it all, the comfortable feeling that comes when healthy young appetites have been pleasantly satisfied.

If you were to get out your dictionaries and look up the derivation of the word "lady," you would discover that it has evolved from the Old English "hlaefdige;" "hlaef," meaning loaf and "dig," to knead, as of dough. A lady then is, literally, a loaf kneader, a bread maker. And so ladies, if you wish, get out your "dough dish;" scatter the flour, warm the milk, and soften the yeast until it reaches the foaming brim; blend with the flour; push, roll, turn, and knead the resilient mixture; watch it rise and punch it down; pat and shape and mold and watch it rise again; let your oven do its work. And then, when the golden loaves are knocked free of the baking tins, tap for the hollow sound on bottom and sides. Fill your kitchen with the most delectable of odours and, surely, in your households, all will be right with the world.

A Wood Splitter's Reverie

1978

The coming of the short days and cold nights has meant that I have to give more attention now to the care and feeding of my old iron kitchen stove. This winter's wood arrived a little late this year and I'm barely keeping ahead of the splitting game. A fine Saturday morning finds me at the woodpile, axe in hand, prepared to furnish a week's supply all at once. But if it's stormy, or if there are other demands on time, I have to utilize the waning light of late afternoons or even the pale glow from the partial moon.

Whenever it is, I still find splitting wood a pleasurable occupation after a sedentary day. The crisp, clear air gets down to the bottom of your lungs as your muscles warm to the task, and there's a certain satisfaction in meeting the challenge of knotty pieces to break the general monotony of swing and slice. It's also very pleasant to be out of doors on a crisp cold morning, to see the sunlight illumine the bare trees or gleam from the river ice and, if it's in the afternoon, to watch the distinctive December evening suffuse the clouds and the hills before the creeping shadows banish the roseate glow completely. I understand that more and more New Brunswickers are rediscovering the aesthetic and therapeutic benefit of this ancient form of exercise, as wood has returned to popularity as a source of household heat.

The other day, I was reading about the old iron works which operated at several periods during the last half of the 19th century, producing pig iron from a smelter situated on the south bank of Lane's Creek, just below my place here on the river. The iron was originally carted to the railway terminus at Richmond, near St. Andrews, and then went by ship to England where it was used for the cladding of British battleships of the Royal Navy. The charcoal required for the operation was prepared in nearby kilns, and I remember that what seemed like a very large supply of hardwood was required for the operation. In 1864, for example, it was estimated that they would require 12,000 cords. It would keep 150 men busy for 12 weeks to cut the wood as well as 60 men and their teams for the same length of time to haul it.

The cost of this wood was not listed in the account I read but I've heard old timers say that their grandparents delivered wood to the old iron works for as little as a dollar a cord. And that's a far cry from present prices. I trust that the return of wood delivered to private households will not be accompanied by a revival of some of the practices the old-timers also told me about — ways of making a load of wood seem much larger than it actually was. I wondered whether such a practice gave to one Carleton County resident the welcome by which he was generally known. They called him "Short Cord" (and let's make it "Short Cord Anonymous" in case he was innocent.)

One summer day some 20 years ago, this gentleman was helping Bill Hamilton, who rented some of our fields, with his haying operation. My wife, Dees, happened to drop in at Bill's place when he and Short Cord were on the lawn transferring a load of hay from the wagon to the mow. A large hay fork suspended from a beam would be lowered into the load, Short Cord would grab the rope and jump on the fork with both feet to lock it into place, jump off again, and then Bill would back up his truck to raise the fork full up to the block from which it would move in over the mow. Then, Bill would climb up, tip the fork and let his hay fall. When he saw Dees, Bill said, "You're just in time, we need someone to back up in the truck."

Dees agreed to help, but being a little concerned about her inexperience, she raised the first load or two rather slowly. As the fork sank into the hay for the third time, Dees heard Bill call, "Come on, you'll have to move faster than that." So she stepped on the gas rather suddenly and did speed up until she heard a roar from Bill which caused her to brake automatically. When she turned around to see what was happening, there was poor Short Cord both feet still on the hay fork, clinging frantically to the rope, his head about two inches away from the barn beam. Dees says that despite the danger, the poor fellow looked so ludicrous swinging back and forth up there that she just had to put her head down over the wheel and laugh, so that it was a minute or two before she could let him down.

Well, this is the random way one's mind and one's memory seem to operate while the axe whirls through the air and the split pieces fall on a sunny morning or a twilit afternoon.

Remembrance Day

1979

Here in New Brunswick, as we near the hour of remembrance, we plan to pay our annual tribute to those who fought and died in the Boer War, two World Wars, and the Korean War. It might be well to remember, too, that in an earlier time wives lost husbands and mothers lost sons, as men fought and died to preserve the British North American colonies that later became confederated as the Dominion of Canada.

I would like to read this morning from a memorial, or request, written on the 12th of April in the year 1816, and preserved in the pages of a Woodstock paper, *The Carleton Sentinel*,[66] printed on the 17th of September 1850:

> To the Right Honourable the Secretary of War.
>
> The memorial of Elizabeth Hopkins, wife of Jeremiah Hopkins, Serjeant of the 104th (New Brunswick) Regiment of Foot.
>
> Most humbly sheweth;
>
> That she was born of British parents at Philadelphia, in the year 1741; has her husband, six sons, and a son-in-law, viz. Jeremiah Hopkins (husband), Samuel Woodward, Timothy Woodward, Robert Woodward, Nathaniel Woodward, Archibald Woodward, Richard Hopkins (sons), James McDonough (son-in-law), serving his Majesty in the 104th; and during the course of her life, from her zeal and attachment to her king and country, she has encountered more hardships than usually fall to the lot of her sex.

66 A weekly newspaper published in Woodstock, NB from 1848-1943, then continued under the name *The Sentinel Press* until 1971.

That in the year 1776, being with her first husband (John Jasper), a Serjeant of marines, on board the brig Stanley, tender to the Roebuck, she was wounded in her left leg, in an engagement with three French vessels, when she was actually working at the guns.

That the marines having been landed at Cape May, in America, her husband was taken prisoner by a Captain Plunkett, of the rebel army, near Mud-Fort Nied, and sentenced to suffer death;

That by her means he was enabled to escape, with 22 American deserters, to whom she served arms and ammunition; and on their way to join the army their party was attacked by the enemy's light horse; she was fired at, and wounded in her left arm; but, undismayed, took a loaded firelock, shot the rebel, and brought his horse to Philadelphia (the head-quarters of the army),which she was permitted to sell to one of General Sir William Howe's Aide-de-Camps.

That after many fatigues and campaigns, her first husband died, and she married Samuel Woodward, a soldier in Colonel Chambers' corps; was with the troops under General Campbell, taken at Pensacola, having, during the siege, served at the guns, and tore her very clothes for wadding.

That having been exchanged at the peace of 1783, from attachment to the royal cause, she was embarked on board a transport with part of de Lancey's and Chambers' troops, was shipwrecked on Seal Island in the Bay of Fundy, when near three hundred men, and numbers of women and children were lost;

That she suffered unparalleled hardship, being pregnant, and with a child in her arms; remained three days on the wreck; was taken up with her husband and child

> by fishermen off Marble-head and shortly after being landed, delivered of three sons; two of whom are in the 104th, the other dead;
>
> Lastly, that she had the honour of being mother of 22 children, viz. 18 sons and four daughters, seven of the former being alive, and three of the latter.
>
> That your memorialist humbly prays, that you may consider her as a fit object for some allowance from the compassionate fund, toward her maintenance in her old age, having lost all her property, and as a reward for her long and faithful services to her king.
>
> Fredericton, New Brunswick, 12th April 1816.

The Sentinel article continues:

> The following is another instance of her strength of mind: at Sacket's Harbour the pride of her heart, her twins, fell: also McDonough, her son-in-law. On hearing the news, she called her children around her, made them an animated speech, charged them to be revenged on the Yankees for their loss; and next time they went into action they were cheered and encouraged by Mammy Hopkins, the name she went by in the regiment.

Mrs. Hopkins received the requested provision. I'm sure that she would be pleased if she knew that on this November 11th some of us will pay a silent tribute to the memory of her twin sons and her son-in-law and other young New Brunswickers who fought and died in the War of 1812, and for whom there is no tangible monument in their native province.[67]

---

67 The Government of Canada erected a plaque in Officer's Square in Fredericton, NB commemorating the winter march of the 104th Regiment from Fredericton to Kingston, ON from where they journeyed to participate in the raid on Sackets Harbour, NY on May 29, 1813.

Thoughts Regarding Indian Artifacts

1981

A few evenings ago just before sunset, I was splitting some kindling out in the yard and generally tidying up the place. As I carried an armful into the house, I noticed that, in a corner of the front step, there was a little pile of flint chippings and rude Indian artifacts that I had picked up along the shore during summertime periods of low water. After unloading the kindling, I went back to retrieve the pieces and take them into the house. I had walked up and down the shore only twice this summer, and not very far at that, so my find was limited: chippings of different kinds of stone, a half-finished arrowhead that had obviously been abandoned by its maker because he didn't like the way it was progressing, and a red jasper hide scraper, irregular in shape, but definitely usable for its designed purpose, and with expert secondary chipping along its serrated edges.

My walks along the shore were intended to be just that, walks along the shore. But, since the days when I used to accompany my late father-in-law, Dr. G.F. Clarke, on his spare-time searches for relics of our prehistoric past, I find that my eyes automatically examine the eroded shoreline and silty beach. Whenever I reach to pick up an arrowhead, a knife, a scraper, or even a chip, my walk no longer seems to be solitary. I can almost hear Dr. Clarke at my elbow saying, "Good lad. That's a fine example. Be sure to note exactly where you found it." He was a man who derived great pleasure from his avocation and, as he said in his book *Someone Before Us*,

> The doing of anything for the pure love of it, which adds to our knowledge and does no harm to anyone, has its own reward. Especially is this true in that branch of archaeology which deals with the Stone Age. It takes me out of doors beside brooks and rivers, along

> intervale lands and terraces, where primitive man had his temporary wigwam or more permanent palisaded village. It trains the eye, makes for good health and an appreciation of all phases of nature.
>
> When I am tired of walking or digging, I sit and watch the river rippling over the shallows and around the heads of islands. I am interested in everything; in the little spotted sandpiper running along the beach, stopping often to bob and bow; in the kingfisher as it plummets, a symphony of blue and white, into the pellucid depth of a pool in which its sharp eyes have detected some small form of fish life. I am interested in the wild flowers; the blood root, arbutus, violet, the linnaea, the wild rose — all the galaxy of beauty that blooms from early spring until late autumn.[68]

That interest was Dr. Clarke's legacy to many of his friends and his readers.

Another thing about the finding of artifacts along the river is the spur it gives to the imagination. You can't handle a piece without wondering about the man who made it, and your mind becomes filled with images of wigwams and campfires and summer fields of maize and birch bark canoes and all other attributes of an ancient way of life. The other evening, holding that red jasper scraper in my hands, I was conscious of the continuity of human existence over the centuries and of man's small victories over time.

I banked the fire in the old iron stove and went out to drive down to the Clarke house. But before I left, I stood for a few minutes by the river bank. Downstream, the smooth water mirrored the last of the sunset flanked by the green glow of twilight and, upriver, a broad band of brilliance led toward the full moon rising over Sharp's Mountain. The chill November air promised another night of frost and a morning skim of ice on the pond. I knew that in the olden days it would be time

---

68 From the author's introduction to the book. Homer assisted in the editing of the work.

for the Indian people to break camp at the village, separate into small hunting parties, and leave the river until the coming of another spring. I remember thinking, so aware of the remote past and standing there in the spell of the timeless moonlight, that I hoped the coming winter would be a mild one.

Praise For November

1979

I think you will have to agree that this year, the month of November has lived up to all my claims in defense of it. In spite of a succession of rainy Saturdays and an above average supply of moisture generally, there have been some very pleasant moments in between. I have listened to more weather conversation couched in incredulous terms this month than for many a year, as coatless pedestrians soaked up the sunshine of balmy afternoons and compared notes on fuel consumption. But the chief visual pleasure of the lingering season has been in watching the ever-changing appearance of the sky overhead. There has been such variety in the combinations of cloud and sunlight this November as to make one realize why Shelley[69] wrote his long poem about the cloud, or why author Guy Murchie described clouds in the following extravagant terms:

> If winds are the spirit of the sky's ocean, the clouds are its texture. They are embodied imagination, the sheet music of the heavens, the architecture of moving air. Theirs is easily the most uninhabited dominion of the earth. Nothing in physical shape is too fantastic for them. They can be as round as apples or as fine as string, as dense as a jungle, as wispy as a whiff of down, as mild as puddle water, or as potent as the belch of a volcano. Some are thunderous anvils formed by violent updrafts from the warm earth. Some are ragged coat-tails of storms that have passed. Some are stagnant blankets of warm air resting on cold. Some are mare's tails floating in the chill upper sky. Some are herring-bones, sheets,

69 Percy Bysshe Shelley (1792-1822), English poet, author of *The Cloud* (1820).

> cream puffs, ox-bends, veils, hammerheads, spangled mantillas, sponges, black shrouds.[70]

Mr. Murchie would certainly have seen all these and more in the skies above Carleton County during the last 30 days. There have been extra dividends too since the rivers and lakes and streams have remained largely ice free, and the water birds have postponed their migrations. Under the cloud cover over the river, the white wings of gulls and terns still beat the still air or catch the autumn winds. Long "vees" of Canada geese have been moving with the dawn from the river's haven to combined grain fields inland and back again with the day's last light, gabbling in their indescribable language which always seem to strike a note of contagious excitement. And even the occasional heron was still to be seen and heard, great wings flapping and long legs outstretched to form a kind of oriental silhouette against the darkening sky.

Just the other afternoon, shortly before sunset time, I stood by the river and looked upward. It had rained earlier in the day and there were still black banners of storm moving over the eastern hill. But directly over the water, the clouds had thinned and grey beams of filtered light shone through, fanning out from a single point behind the general overcast. To the west there were blue breaks, and separate cloud masses were topped with gold and silver, the whole panorama moving and shifting and changing rapidly as the west wind blew — not a wild west wind, but brisk enough for all that.

At this time last year there was snow on the ground, and no one can tell what November will be like in 1980. But odds are better than even that a time will come when weather-conscious conversationalists will be saying, "Do you remember the November we had back in '79?"

---

70 Guy Murchie (1907-97), American author, journalist, pilot, and flight instructor. From *Song of the Sky* (1954).

The Canada Goose

1976

A few days ago, I was driving up the river road toward home about sunset time when I saw a "vee" of some 30 wild geese wheel inland from over the river. It was a grey day of heavy overcast and the great birds were black against the cloud curtain. The formation shifted sometimes when individuals changed position but there was no real variation to the traditional pattern. Whether they meant to break their journey for the night as gleaners in a recently harvested grain field, or whether they would swing back over the river again, I didn't know, but I felt the customary thrill of excitement that always accompanies the sight of migrating flocks. Being in the car, I couldn't hear the sound of their voices as they passed over the road and swiftly disappeared from view.

When I got home, I asked my wife if she had seen them. She said, "No," but she told me that the night before when she had been down at her mother's in town, she had heard a flight go over. There was some light in the night sky but a heavy mist veiled the face of the full moon and they couldn't be seen. For some time, though, she listened to the indescribable sound of a large flock in full choir and she, too, felt once again an emotional response to their constant clamouring.

Last Christmastime, our son Stephen, who was home for the holidays, noticed in the snow on the pond ice the tracks of a big bird, and then he saw a Canada goose which had missed the migration and was in obvious trouble. He tried to catch it but the bird had enough strength to struggle into the air and fly away. We put out a pile of grain on the ice, hoping the goose would find it if it should return. For several days there was no sign of it but, in the week between Christmas and New Year's, we noticed that the grain had been disturbed and a further search disclosed the goose out on the river ice.

Stephen and our next-door neighbour's daughter, Jane, who was also home for the holidays, ran out after it and, this time, the bird was so weak that Stephen managed to capture it. He wrapped his jacket around it and carried it to the house where we found a warm place for it and were encouraged when it tried to take a little sustenance. I made a large cage for the goose from the summer window screens and we hoped that we could nurse it back to the point where it could be taken to the south coast of the province, since several wintering geese had been observed there. But it was not to be. Malnutrition and dehydration had gone too far and the goose, unfortunately, did not survive.

What is there about this particular species that has such an appeal for people, apart from the nationalism of the name itself? The tendency of many is to assess even wildlife in human terms, and I suppose there is a kind of puritan approval of the monogamous habits of Canada geese, who eschew promiscuity and mate for life. Then, if you apply a political criterion, you could say that geese combine the small "c" conservative elements of stability and continuity with small "l" liberal characteristics of freedom and self-determination, and there are some overtones of socialist planning for their migration journeys.

In a world where environmental pressures are obviously endangering the continued existence of so much wildlife that we have traditionally taken for granted, it is comforting to know that, for the present at least, we can count on seeing and hearing, in early spring and late fall, the dramatic flights of Canada geese en route to or from their wintering places. There are few who would dismiss their passing with just a casual glance, for their trumpetings tell of the splendours of the natural world that is our heritage, and remind each of us of our responsibilities in the problems of its preservation.

And when you watch the ordered passage of the great flocks, reflecting the life force in the relentless beating of powerful wings, there is a subconscious surge of sympathy, welling from something wild and free in the depths of the human spirit, responding to the beginning or the end of another season.

“This is Ken Homer
in Upper Woodstock.”

Discovering the Important Things of Life

A Memoir

When I was an organic farmer, growing vegetables on one of the remaining tracts of farmland on Montreal's West Island, an event occurred that brought my father, Ken Homer, vividly to mind. This was a few years after his death in 2003.

Stephen and Ken Homer at the farm, 1957. (EKH)

Every summer my Community-Supported Agriculture customers, who received weekly vegetable baskets, would participate in a work bee at the farm, weeding, picking potatoes, or performing any other task that was needed. At the end of the work bee we would have a picnic.

On this occasion a group of us were having our lunch on a grassy knoll overlooking the fields. Jim and Liz Taylor, then in their early 80s, were seated on aluminum lawn chairs. Conversation had turned to our personal lives and I enquired of Jim, a renowned academic at l'Université de Montréal, where he had gone to university.

"Mount Allison so fair," he replied.

"Oh," I said. "My father studied there and then taught English for a year in the late 40s."

"His name," asked Jim.

"Ken, Ken Homer," I replied.

"Ken Homer!" cried Jim as he threw his arms over his head. The gesture tipped the lawn chair backward, and he tumbled head over heels down the knoll. We scrambled to get him up and once back in his chair he said fervently, "Ken Homer was the best teacher I ever had."

Over the years I have become accustomed to hearing compliments about my father: as a teacher from former high school students, as a radio and television broadcaster who captivated listeners with his poetic language and the timbre of his voice, and as a poised and gentle man who imparted his knowledge with grace and wit. It seemed that the depth of his knowledge and his sincerity of interest in the lives of people both modest and great was passed easily to his students, even those who admitted to being less than stellar academically.

I only witnessed my father as a history teacher in Grade 11 at the Woodstock High School. Although I remember him as genial and at ease, at that age having one's father as a teacher was a slight embarrassment and difficult to critically appreciate.

Ken Homer, Halifax. Born 1915. (EKH)

My dad, Kenneth Churchill Homer, grew up in Yarmouth, Nova Scotia, a fog-bound town on the province's south shore. He had two brothers and a sister. His dad, Murray, was a shopkeeper, his mother, Jane, lived to the age of 101.

I know little of my dad's childhood. He spoke infrequently of his family and seemed reluctant to be in regular contact. I remember only one visit to Yarmouth to visit my grandmother.

Alcohol seemed to have played a destructive role on the male side of the family. His father died relatively young. His younger brother committed suicide in mid-life, and his other brother was a restless wanderer. His mother was described to me as being cool and remote, although I don't remember her that way from my visit. To me, there always seemed to be an aura of sadness enveloping the Yarmouth side of the family.

Ken Homer at Mount Allison University, late 1930s. (EKH)

Ken became the academic and the athlete in the family. He thrived on academics, especially literature. He spent several summers as a YMCA counsellor. At Mount Allison University, he was as adept at debating and editing the school newspaper (*The Argosy*) as he was on the football pitch and basketball court. He was also a gymnast and a terrific dancer.

As a senior in 1938 he met and fell in love with Mary Clarke who was attending the Mount Allison Ladies College. "Dees," her nickname from infancy, was from Woodstock, New Brunswick. She was pretty, vivacious, creative, and artistic. She was clever but not academically inclined.

She fell head over heels for Ken, and he for her—with some reservations. Ken was enchanted by Dees, even though she suffered mental repercussions from an attack of encephalitis and ensuing paralysis at the age of two. She recovered and relearned to walk, but the illness seemed to have had continuing effects. As a young person, Dees was impulsive, at times depressed, cleverly manipulative, and had bouts of rage when her way was thwarted.

Ken & Dees. (EKH)

Dees brought Ken to visit Woodstock. Ken fell under the spell of the Clarke family, and, it must be said, they were completely taken by him. The Clarke family must have seemed the polar opposite to his. They were interested in literature, history, and natural history. Dees's father, George Frederick Clarke, was opinionated and passionate: a dentist, a writer of poetry, historical novels, and tales of natural history. He was a keen amateur archaeologist intent on mapping the past of New Brunswick's Indigenous peoples. Dees's mother, Mary, was calm, warm, and welcoming. Her sister Jane was funny and a talented musician training to be a concert pianist. The Clarke household immediately embraced Ken.

In 1939, as war with Germany threatened, Dees pressed for marriage. Ken waffled, in love but with creative ambitions of his own and a growing awareness that Dees could be a handful. In September, when Canada did declare war, Dees skipped out of Woodstock and landed on Ken's doorstep in London, Ontario where he had a summer job. They married on September 18, 1939.

Ken & Dees wedding, 1939. (EKH)

From the beginning, their visions clashed; Dees wanted children and to live close to her parents. She was emotional, romantic and envisaged an agrarian life beside the St. John River. Ken, only 24, had graduated with honours and wanted to launch a career in teaching and writing. On the emotional scale he was warm and charming, but according to Dees, frustratingly lacking in demonstrations of affection. For their first 17 years of marriage they lived apart more than together.

Nonetheless, in 1945, in an act that ultimately would bind them together, and with financial help from Dees's father, they bought an 1830s white clapboarded farmhouse on an intervale along the banks of the St. John River a few miles north of Woodstock. It was a small world apart, nestled between a steep wooded hill on one side and the swiftly flowing river on the other.

The Farmhouse in winter. (EKH)

A winding lane led to the valley highway. It was idyllic and verdant, alive with birdsong. Each spring the flat produced an abundant crop of fiddleheads and the wooded hillside was carpeted in yellow dog-toothed violets and red trilliums. In the fall, it glowed with the colours of basswood, maple, and ironwood. Fields of corn and pasture land with grazing Holstein cows led to the nearest neighbour, dairy farmer Robert Speer, a mile up the flat.

Dees and Ken spent one happy summer at the farm, as it became known. They had a garden, goats, and a cow named Daisy. Ken and a colleague from Lower Canada College ran an outdoor summer school for some of their high school students. But in the fall of 1946 Ken was offered a position teaching English at Mount Allison University. It was exactly what he wanted and he accepted.

His departure upset and enraged Dees, her vision for their future thwarted. She launched into an affair with Ken's brother, Leonard, who had landed in Woodstock after fighting with the Canadian army in Italy. From the reading of family letters, it was clear that Len was more emotional and less ambitious than Ken. Profoundly distressed,

Ken did not renew his Mount Allison teaching post and spent a year as a farmworker in Wiltshire, England.

In the fall of 1947 Len broke off the affair. Dees became unstable and suicidal; her parents sought professional help and she was put under the care of a Boston psychiatrist. She was diagnosed as "a borderline personality." For the next five years she spent summers at the farm and the rest of the year in Boston, in and out of the psychiatric ward of Massachusetts General Hospital.

Ken Homer. Photo by Mike Saunders. (CCHS)

In 1948 Ken returned to Canada to take a job as a broadcaster with the CBC in Halifax. His career blossomed. It was the early days of television broadcasting and the CBC had a mandate to show Canada to Canadians. From 1948 to 1955 Ken wrote scripts and narrated programs about people and places across the country. Many of the broadcasts were "live" and Ken, verbally adept and with an instinctive sense of presentation, became known as a consummate broadcaster.

During this time, Dees and Ken, separated but still married and still holding onto flickerings of love, spent his summer holidays together at the farm in Upper Woodstock.

In 1952, while still in psychiatric treatment in Boston, Dees had a brief affair with a young painter. It ended, but unknown to the young painter, Dees had become pregnant. She returned to Woodstock determined to keep the baby. I was born in February 1953.

For the next two years I lived with my mother and grandparents in Woodstock. My true parentage was confused by my mother who had one story for close family and another for the rest of the world—

Dees, Ken, & Stephen in Halifax, Chrismas 1956. (EKH)

including me. When rumours circulated and schoolmates teased me in my early teens I confronted Ken and Dees who presented me with a birth certificate showing Ken as father and with a united story of their secret rendezvous and my conception in an historic inn in Concord, Massachusetts.

What is clear from discussions with my older relatives is that after my birth Dees became happy and more emotionally stable. In January 1956 she flew to Halifax and made an impassioned pitch to reunite our little family. Ken was already seeing someone else, but amazingly he accepted. What made him put aside a new romance, so many past battles, infidelities, and hurt we will never know. Years later I asked him why? He acknowledged the difficulties and challenges but simply said, "I always loved the little bugger."

Of his love for Dees I have no doubt, but I also suspect that his deep, innate kindness foresaw the difficulties that could lie ahead for a small boy with a fragile mother and he took the noblest of actions.

Our family reunited in Halifax for one year. One of my earliest memories is having a bit role in a program about the Nova Scotia giants, Annie Swan and Angus MacAskill, where I opened the program by sitting on my father's knee and asking, "Daddy, are there really giants?"

Ken Homer, summer 1964. (Photo by Ian Fleming)

After a year in Halifax, Dees tired of the city and persuaded Ken once again to move to the farm where she was sure he could have a successful career as a freelancer. Notwithstanding an offer to be a lead broadcaster in Toronto and another offer as a correspondent in London, England, Ken agreed to make the farm his home.

In a reflection on his choice to move from city to country, and in response to those who questioned how creative work could be done in such a quiet rural atmosphere, Ken once said, "Creative work is nothing more than a sharing of creative ideas and emotional responses to the important things of life itself. I'm just beginning to discover what mine are."

While our family settled into year-round life at the farmhouse on the bank of the St. John River, Ken continued to receive work assignments that took him all over Canada. In 1958 he covered the Springhill Mine disaster and was the only remaining media person at the pithead when the last miners were brought out, against all hope, alive. He covered Queen Elizabeth's Royal Canadian tour. He was the television host for the Calgary Stampede. He emceed the Miramichi Folksong Festival for years, not only introducing performers but also keeping them sober before show time.

However, his most creative work, and that which I believe gave him the most satisfaction, was doing the radio essays called "Away From It All," a series that chronicled our move from city to country. (These radio essays from the 1950s and '60s pre-date those found in this

Ken in the garden. (EKH)

volume.) The creation of these radio essays allowed him the freedom to observe and reflect entirely on his own terms. Our country life was a tableau; our family and the coterie of animals were the cast.

Our daily lives became the fodder for his essays. Each season had its rituals and he mused about them all. For example, he wrote about the late February tapping of the large maple at the top of our tree-lined driveway, the boiling down of sap to syrup, the late November collecting of spruce boughs to insulate the foundation of our wood heated farmhouse, the splitting of hardwood blocks, the stacking of the firewood in our dirt floor basement, my mother's learning how to bake her marvellous pies in "Pandora," the large McClary wood-burning kitchen stove.

When a hunter friend gave us some venison, the ensuing production of mincemeat became a family project, my father cutting the flank into cubes, my mother preparing the ingredients, and four year old me turning the handle of the meat grinder. The final step was his radio script on making mincemeat that emerged the following week.

The flat & the farmhouse, spring freshet, 1956. (EKH)

The cannon-like booms of the river ice cracking and breaking up in the lengthening days of spring, the unleashing of the ice cakes the size of city blocks, and the resulting freshet was a powerful natural marvel in which Ken delighted, even though for a few days every April we were house-bound. The roiling waters of the St. John River freshet covered the flat and surrounded our house, the only exit being a paddle in the Chestnut canoe from our front steps to the edge of the hillside driveway.

One autumn we had a roaring chimney fire. My dad reacted swiftly but calmly, climbed a ladder to the roof and poured buckets of old stove ash down the chimney, which suffocated the fire. The event became a reminder to country neophytes that stovepipes must have the creosote removed annually. His description of this arduous process became one of his most appreciated radio broadcasts.

All the comings and goings of the animal life that populated our intervale were observed, noted, and included in his radio musings: the red fox pouncing on mice hidden under the snow, the red-breasted nuthatch creeping head first down the butternut tree by the side of the house, the bald eagles that built their nest on Pine Island a mile up river. He was not a born naturalist — but he became one. And for the first time in years my mother and father were in harmony, they worked as a team; those were the best years of their lives.

My mother learned the skills of a country housewife. She made jams and pickles and dealt with the wintry challenges of an outhouse and bathing in a galvanised washtub. She pulled roasts, baked beans, cakes, and pies from the oven of the wood-fired kitchen stove and generally transferred her romantic vision of country living seamlessly into a pragmatic, no-nonsense reality.

Dees Homer. (Photo by Ian Fleming)

Then, secure in personal life, she launched herself, and all those around her, into her new avocation — the creation of the Carleton County Historical Society. The main purpose of this ambitious project was to bring alive the history of our shire and to restore to its former magnificence the local county courthouse which had been used as a horse barn for the past fifty years.

Dees was a force of nature, but now in a dynamic and positive way. She came up with fundraising ideas like an annual salmon fry and a period costume ball. She dreamed up mini-stage productions

Carleton County Historical Society Salmon Fry, Upper Woodstock.
Ken Homer, Charles Gardiner, & Ken Perley (EKH)

Ken, Dees, & Stephen dressed for the CCHS Costume Ball. (EKH)

to illustrate local historical events for which Ken wrote the theatre scripts. She enlisted anyone and everyone in the county to participate. She badgered the provincial government for grants to restore the old courthouse. She found Canada's best restoration architect, Peter John Stokes, who helped guide the courthouse restoration.

Dees was the creative director, the background driving force of this community-based project. He was the speech giver, the President of the Board, and public persona of the Historical Society. Our kitchen table became the hub of all this activity, from pickle-making projects, to planning sessions for meetings of the Historical Society, to tea and cookies with TV producers who came to work with my dad on planning TV broadcasts.

And there was me. It's not immodest to say that I added glue to the family structure. I was, of course, too young to hear or appreciate my

Ken & Stephen go fishing. (EKH)

father's radio broadcasts, but as I listen to them now — having had them transcribed from his reel to reel tapes to CDs by the Provincial Archives of New Brunswick — I realize how much pleasure he took in observing the budding curiosity of a young boy. I now realize how fortunate I was to have been raised in this place, during this period of their otherwise fraught lives, by this animated mother and this gentle father.

With my mother coaxing him out of his inner reflections into fatherhood duty, he became a quiet and calm companion in the daily rituals of country living. The drudgery of piling heavy, splintery birch and maple rounds from the woodpile would, at his suggestion, become the delight of caching bars of precious metals safely in our castle dungeon.

Every spring he would report to me the arrival of the first Song Sparrow, and I would report to him the arrival of the Mourning Cloak butterfly. In May, we would trek off to nearby Lane's Creek to fish trout, only keeping enough for a mid-day meal. When I was old enough to hunt but still required adult accompaniment, he, who took no pleasure in killing but recognized the teenage rite of passage I sought, agreed to come with me and even to carry a shotgun, though he always passed the option of shooting a partridge or duck to me and never once fired.

My father entertained the small pleasures of each season but especially of plunging into the extremes of winter. He and I had a ritual of an after-dark walk on Christmas Eve across the fields to our neighbours, the Speers, a mile up river. My mother would go by car bearing her traditional gift of an angel food cake. If the night sky was clear my father would point out the Big Dipper, the Little Dipper, Orion, and the

Ken & Stephen in winter. (EKH)

Ken & Dees watching a television program about the Macatquac Dam, summer 1964. (Photo by Mary Bernard)

North Star. If it was a blizzard, we put our heads down, and ploughing through blinding snow, one of us would always say to the other, "Don't you love blizzards?"

In 1964, the construction of the Mactaquac hydroelectric dam was announced. It was to be built 20 kilometres upriver from Fredericton and would create a nearly one-hundred-kilometre-long headpond stretching to a few kilometres up river from our farm. It was a project touted to provide 20 percent of the province's electricity and power economic development well into the future. But it would also flood some of the best farmland in the province, displace hundreds of farm families, flood Indigenous gravesites, and destroy much of the St. John River watershed as a major North American habitat for Atlantic salmon.

My mother responded with her trademark passion and energy, forming The Association for the Preservation of the St. John River in its Natural State. Ken was seconded to plan strategy, and write protest briefs and speeches. They researched other hydroelectric projects across North America, they sorted out environmental opinions, and they organised petitions and protests.

During this time, my father did infrequent and then finally no broadcast work. My parents refused the ridiculously low buyout

The St. John River at the flats before flooding by the Mactaquac Dam. (EKH)

offered by the New Brunswick Electric Power Commission. After Power Commission negotiators were greeted by Dees holding a shotgun they ceased to visit. The property was expropriated.

By 1967 the fight against the dam was lost and the river valley from Mactaquac to above Upper Woodstock was flooded. At the farm, the swift running river was replaced by a deep and still headpond. There were no more salmon or shad running in the river. Motorboats raced by. My mother was crushed. After a scant eight years of hectic happiness for our little family, our idyllic farm was taken from us.

In the ensuing years we rented a house in the village of Upper Woodstock where we spent our winters only to return each summer to "camp" in the farmhouse that had been expropriated but not yet flooded. In 1969, with our family deep in debt, my father took a job teaching history at the Woodstock High School.

Ice on the St. John River. (EKH)

At some point in the early '70s an exceptionally high spring freshet flooded the house and ice cakes knocked it off its stone foundation. My mother, as though enraged by a misbehaving river, overran my father's call to good sense and insisted on having the house put back on its foundations and made livable for the summer months.

A few years later, when I was at university, another spring flood battered the house. There was no money to fix it. The house remained a broken shell slumping a bit more every year. Strangers arrived by motorboat and rummaged through our belongings that hadn't been removed.

This final loss was accompanied by the return of my mother's old demons. Slowly, the physical effects of encephalitis returned; her feet twisted, her back bent, she got by on painkillers. Her mind was sharp as a tack, and she saw the courthouse restoration to its completion, but she became bitter and self-focused.

My father's high school teaching was his salvation, and in the evenings he once again began doing radio essays, selections of which are found in the present volume. These essays were less about observations derived from our family's experiences of country living and more on general topics of natural and cultural history. He produced meditations on weather, apples, molasses, and baked beans, or, for example, an analysis of harvest from ancient to contemporary times.

He also created vignettes about New Brunswick historical events and notable personages.

He also took on a caretaker role for a few people with whom he shared a love of the past, or an easy and sympathetic emotional connection. This is the kind of relationship he enjoyed with Peter Paul, a member of the Maliseet First Nation community at Lower Woodstock.

Peter Paul, July 1978.
(Photo by Mary Bernard)

Peter Paul was raised primarily by his grandmother. He was familiar with traditional Maliseet customs and stories. He was skilled at making snowshoes and ash-splint baskets. He was adept at fishing and harvesting fiddleheads. He was fluent in Maliseet and researched the language. Peter Paul was my father's kind of man; an intellectual, but without a formal education. He was curious and an avid reader of history. Like my father, he was a man who all his life valued physical activity as much as scholarly study. And, again, like my father, he was gentle and kind, a man of integrity.

In the summer of 1967, when it was clear that the Mactaquac Dam would be built, my parents arranged a canoe trip on the St. John River from Beechwood to Pokiok, a distance of 100 kilometres. We were four: Peter Paul, my father, Robert John Speer, my close neighbour friend three years my senior, and me.

The goal was simple; for us young people to have the experience of canoeing a flowing, undammed river with a man of wisdom. The effect, I suspect, was even deeper for my father. With firelight and shadows dancing on their faces, he and Peter talked and talked late into the nights; talked about the river, its history, its animals, and the stories of the characters that peopled it. Robert John and I fought sleep, straining to catch the stories punctuated by Peter's deep, gentle laugh.

Preparing for the canoe trip from Beachwood to Pokiok.
Ken Homer, Peter Paul, R.J. Speer, and Stephen Homer, 1967. (EKH)

For the next 22 years, until Peter died in 1989, my father and Peter collaborated and shared thoughts about history and humanity over countless cups of tea. They were equally admiring of each other. My father recorded hours of interviews with Peter. When Peter was awarded an honorary degree from the University of New Brunswick, my father appointed himself as his chauffeur and drove him to Fredericton, somewhat afraid that the shy and humble man might decide at the last minute not to go.

As it happened, Peter turned up late at our house putting at risk his arrival at UNB. "Where have you been?" cried my mother in panic. "To the dump. I found my dress shoes," Peter chuckled. He showed her a pair of fairly decent black patent leathers. He put them on, they got in the car, and drove to the convocation.

Another strong emotional connection in my father's life was his mother-in-law, Mary Clarke, Mrs. George Frederick Clarke. She was kind, calm, emotionally restrained, and deeply fond of my father. In 1947, when Ken fled to England, stricken with indecision about his marriage, Mary, or "Mum" as she was called, was his connection to family. They became pen pals of sorts, she writing with news of the comings and goings of the Clarke household, he describing his life on the Wiltshire farm and his rambles about the English countryside.

Ken Homer & Mary Clarke at Crow's Nest. (EKH)

She helped him keep his bearings in this emotionally turbulent time. He and my mother cared for her in her long old age. But it was Ken who took the time to simply be with her, chatting, reading together in the living room, and patiently walking her upstairs to her bedroom. When she finally moved into a seniors' residence he visited her daily until she died at 105.

As the older generation of the Clarke family passed on and Ken and Dees aged, the administration of the Carleton County Historical Society began to change hands. My mother's health and control issues dominated their daily rhythm. It was once again a difficult time, and the image I prefer to carry of my father in his mid-'60s is of him wearing his tweed jacket, recording his radio talks in a small upper bedroom in the G.F. Clarke residence, where they now lived, burying himself in his inner delight of explaining the mundane and the profound. The transcribed radio essays in this book are from this time, the second period of my dad's radio essays.

For my father's funeral in November 2003, we shared a recording that Ken made in 1958, when, as a five year old, I interrupted one of

Ken & Dees at the Old Carleton County Courthouse, June 1986. (EKH)

his taping sessions at the farm. For those who knew him, it reflected the patience and kindness of a good father and the commitment to seek truth as a good teacher. The recording goes like this:

First, the sound of a five-year-old's feet pounding up the stairs to the recording room, interrupting the session. Ken kept the tape rolling and incorporated the interruption in his radio talk.

> Stephen: "Hi Daddy! I didn't find any bugs but I found the shell of a snail. Look! The shell of a snail!"
>
> Ken: "Oh, yes. Was that underneath a board?"
>
> Stephen: "Yes."
>
> Ken: "Well!"
>
> Stephen: "I didn't see any bugs."
>
> Ken: "What kind of bugs are you getting for your collection now?"

Stephen: "Oh, all kinds of bugs. Well, Tiny Mouse [my imaginary friend] says this is the beetle season but when the beetle season is over you don't get any beetles, but maybe next beetle season I might get a another new collection next beetle season. Four more days before beetle season is over—one, two, three, four!"

Ken: "What are you going to collect then?"

Stephen: "Well, worming season comes right after beetle season. I'll get more worms in worming season. But isn't this a nice old snail shell? Where's the snail though?"

Ken: "Well he's gone from that shell."

Stephen: "What happened?"

Ken: "He left the shell behind."

Stephen: "Why did he?"

Ken: "Well, perhaps he died, dear. When they die they just leave the shells behind."

Stephen: "But when they leave their shells that means they die?"

Ken: "Well, they keep their shells on them all their lives."

Stephen: "So this one died?"

Ken: "Hmm, hmm..."

Stephen: "But where is he?"

Ken: "He's all... he's decayed."

Stephen: "What's 'decayed' mean?"

Ken: "Just rotted away and left nothing but the shell behind."

Silent pause.

Stephen: "Well, the shell is very interesting. I'll leave it up here. Everything I get—if I get a bottle and I get a beetle, I'll put him in a bottle and leave him up here."

Ken: "All right, dear."

Stephen: "I'll put it on the shelf here."

Ken: "Bye"

Stephen: "Bye"

Ken: "See you later."

Stephen: "Yeah."

Stephen Homer fishing at Lane's Creek, 1964. (Photo by Mary Bernard)

Footsteps going down the stairs, a little voice is singing, "Wing, zing, ding—beetle oh beetle ..."

Ken continues recording: "I said at the start that the flood was an interruption. Come to think of it, life here is a whole series of interruptions. We stop to hear about Stephen's adventures, we watch the antics of the wild animals playing in the hillside woods or the birds darting among the trees along the riverbank. We take time to see the sunset, or the moonrise over Phillips Mountain."

This is Ken Homer saying so long for now from our old farmhouse on the bank of the St. John River."

Stephen Homer
August 2019

The Artwork

Michael McEwing was commissioned to create the original artwork for the cover and the images for the four title pages which divide the book into seasons.

Like Homer, McEwing is a passionate observer of the natural world. His most recent project, "Conservation on Canvas," an exhibit which toured the province in 2017-18, is a series of large oil paintings depicting features of the preserved areas established by the Nature Trust of New Brunswick.

The wood block print on the cover, featuring a "Homeresque" figure, allows us to observe the observer, drawing us into his activity, and heightening our regard for the natural world. The illustrations inside highlight the delicacy and beauty of that world as it presents itself to us throughout the annual cycle of the seasons, and depict those things that Homer saw and described so aptly for us in his own art form.

Michael McEwing is an art educator with the Anglophone West School District who resides in Woodstock, NB.

The Typeface

This book is set in *Cartier Book*, a digital font based on the *Cartier* typeface, named in honour of Jacques Cartier and presented to Canada by designer Carl Dair (1912-67) in 1967 as part of the country's centennial celebrations.

Dair was a prominent Canadian graphic designer and typographer and *Cartier*, created over a ten-year period, is considered the first Canadian-designed text face. It was used famously for the printing of the widely-distributed poster version of the *Canadian Charter of Rights and Freedoms* in 1982. The typeface, originally produced in only roman and italic, was not readily adaptable to a digital environment, and so fell out of use.

Cartier Book was created by Rod McDonald, a renowned Canadian graphic designer in his own right. He worked to revive the *Cartier* typeface and bring it to a wider contemporary audience. *Cartier Book* was released in 2000, providing functional and highly legible copy text while preserving the artful and distinctive elements of Dair's original design.

The Acknowledgements

It's been a real pleasure to help bring these essays of Ken Homer to print and we are grateful for the generous and enthusiastic support this project has received from so many people.

Herewith, then, our thanks to;

Stephen Homer, for permission, on behalf of the Estate of Ken Homer, to publish the essays; for the wonderful memoir of his father and mother; and for the collection of family photographs it contains;

Mary Bernard, for the striking portraits of Ken Homer, Dees Homer, Peter Paul, and Stephen Homer;

the staff of the Provincial Archives of New Brunswick, for assistance in accessing the Homer papers;

the staff of the New Brunswick Public Library, for help with historical research and reference material;

all those who provided financial support for this publication, including the Carleton County Historical Society; the Town of Woodstock; Lois and John Thompson; Stephen and Kelly Thornton; Wes and Cindy Corey; Barry Craig and Sara MacDonald; Andrea Langdon; Brent Dimock and Sharon Sharpe; Rebecca Harris; Stephen Wilson; David and Marlene Henley; Torrey and Jennifer Sylvester; and Kim Sylvester;

Emily Clark, whose initial suggestion about a volume of Homer's essays was the seed from which this book grew;

Linda Currie, for helpful remembrances concerning the Homers and their Upper Woodstock neighbours;

Michael McEwing, for the beautiful seasonal illustrations and for his inspired woodcut conception of the observed observer;

Chapel Street Editions (CSE), for their continuing work bringing forth books on the history and cultural life of the St. John River Valley;

Brendan Helmuth, for his elegant book design;

Keith and Ellen Helmuth, for their unflagging efforts in support of the mission of CSE and for their warm hospitality on the many evenings this book took shape around their kitchen table;

our dear friends and family (among whom Stephen Kinney warrants special mention), who encouraged this project and offered support as we obsessed over grammatical and textual decisions, and who share our satisfaction in seeing this project come to fruition;

and finally, Ken Homer himself, from whom we learned how much can be gained from walking with a three-legged cat.

SK / RK

The Editors

Stuart Kinney studied history with Ken Homer at Woodstock High School in the mid-1970s. Later, he was among those who enjoyed listening to Homer's weekly radio essays, especially because Stuart had his own three-legged cat.

These encounters left Stuart with an indelible impression concerning Homer's boundless reserves of curious energy and humble grace, and fostered a deep appreciation of his teacher's regard for the natural world and his engagement in his community.

Ross Kinney became familiar with Ken Homer when this project began taking shape in 2017. In a testament to Homer's ability as a writer and storyteller, Ross felt an immediate connection upon reading and hearing these essays. The opportunity to help publish this collection could not be missed

Both Stuart and Ross share Homer's interest in history and literature, and especially in the cultural heritage of western New Brunswick. This kinship, founded on a common bond to Carleton County and the St. John River Valley, grew stronger as this book developed.

Ross attended graduate school at St. John's College in Annapolis, Maryland after studying philosophy and literature at St. Thomas University. He currently lives in Fredericton.

Stuart studied philosophy at the University of King's College, a subject which continues to capture his interest alongside poetry, spirituality and history. He practices law in Woodstock where he resides with his wife, Gloria Yachyshen.

Toward a Vibrant Local Culture

An Afterword

The story behind *Walks With A Three-Legged Cat* demonstrates how close attention to local heritage fosters a vibrant cultural life.

The idea for this book dates to October 2014 and the opening of the Thompson Centre at the L. P. Fisher Public Library in Woodstock, NB. As a local publisher, I was invited to be among the speakers at the opening ceremony. I took the opportunity to announce plans for republishing the books of George Frederick Clarke, a resident of Woodstock and one of New Brunswick's best-known writers during his lifetime. That announcement prompted local history enthusiast Emily Clark to ask, "What about Ken Homer? His radio essays should be published. Ken's writing about life in the St. John River Valley is local literature at its best."

Having heard Ken Homer's radio essays, I thought her suggestion made perfect sense. I was not the only one who thought so. Stuart Kinney came to me that evening expressing his enthusiasm for both the George Frederick Clarke Project and what has now become the Ken Homer Project. Both writers played a significant role in advancing an appreciation for the natural history and cultural heritage of New Brunswick. A book of Ken Homer's selected radio essays would be a perfect addition to Chapel Street Editions' publishing mission.

Stuart Kinney recruited his son Ross, and together they began to work on the book. Its publication at this time can only be explained by recognising the unstinting effort Ross and Stuart brought to this project. If not for their initiative, it would still be on CSE's future agenda. Their editorial management — selecting essays, arranging for illustration, facilitating the association of the Carleton County Historical Society, and securing the book's community-based funding — has been essential to the production of *Walks With A Three-Legged Cat.*

In addition, Stephen Homer's memoir, written for this book, recounts his father's extraordinary qualities of mind and heart, and documents the devotion of his parents to their community and its cultural heritage. And finally, Michael McEwing's illustrations add a dimension of visual delight and reflective pause that mirrors the mind of Ken Homer and the composition of his essays.

Altogether, the collaborative process that created *Walks With A Three-Legged Cat*, along with its literary, biographical, and visual content, is a marker for the irreplaceable value of community-minded cultural life.

Heritage is not an ornament. Individually and in community, it's how we know who we are. Close attention to the natural history and heritage of where we live is the leading edge of a vibrant cultural life. *Walks With a Three-Legged Cat* shows Ken Homer as a true exemplar in this regard.

Keith Helmuth
Publisher & Managing Editor
Chapel Street Editions

www.ingramcontent.com/pod-product-compliance
Lightning Source LLC
Chambersburg PA
CBHW040222170726
48295CB00014B/778

* 9 7 8 1 9 8 8 2 9 9 2 6 6 *